BUILDING THE RESPONSIVE CAMPUS

To Gib Hentschke,
Dean of the School of the Rossier Education
at the University of Southern California,
for his energy, enthusiasm, and desire
for bringing about constructive educational reform.

BUILDING THE RESPONSIVE CAMPUS

Creating
High
Performance
Colleges
and
Universities

William G. Tierney

SAGE Publications
International Educational and Professional Publisher
Thousand Oaks   London   New Delhi

For information:

SAGE Publications, Inc.
2455 Teller Road
Thousand Oaks, California 91320
E-mail: order@sagepub.com

SAGE Publications Ltd.
6 Bonhill Street
London EC2A 4PU
United Kingdom

SAGE Publications India Pvt. Ltd.
M-32 Market
Greater Kailash I
New Delhi 110 048 India

Printed in the United States of America

Library of Congress Cataloging-in-Publication Data

Tierney, William G.
    Building the responsive campus: Creating high performance
colleges and universities / by William G. Tierney.
        p.   cm.
    Includes bibliographical references and index.
    ISBN 0-7619-0987-7 (cloth: acid-free paper)
    ISBN 0-7619-0988-5 (pbk.: acid-free paper)
        1. Universities and colleges—United States—Administration.
    2. Universities and colleges—United States—Faculty.   3. Educational
change—United States.   I. Title.
    LB2341 .T584   1998
    378.1′01—ddc21   98-40068

This book is printed on acid-free paper.

00   01   02   03   04   05   7   6   5   4   3   2

Acquiring Editor:	Jim Nageotte
Editorial Assistant:	Heidi Van Middlesworth
Production Editor:	Diana E. Axelsen
Editorial Assistant:	Stephanie Allen
Typesetter/Designer:	Lynn Miyata
Indexer:	Virgil Diodato
Cover Designer:	Michelle Lee

Contents

Acknowledgments

I am a lucky fellow. I sent this text out for commentary to individuals whom I was certain would take me to task for loose writing or flabby thinking. They did. Their comments forced me to spend a good deal longer on this book than I had originally envisioned, but the book (and I) are better for it. Thanks to Judy Glazer, Michael Jackson, Gail Lin Joe, Kent M. Keith, David Leslie, Yvonna Lincoln, Jack Newell, Bill Segura, Melora Sundt, Dan Tompkins, and three anonymous reviewers. Parker C. Johnson and Mujaji Davis in the Center for Higher Education Policy Analysis helped prepare the text and I am in their debt. I appreciate the help of Kristen Maus in copyediting the text. Jim Nageotte, my editor at Sage, has become a true friend, mentor, and wordsmith.

Much of the work for this book was made possible by generous support from the Pew Charitable Trusts. The opinions, of course, are mine alone.

Introduction

Far and away the best prize that life offers is the chance to work hard at work worth doing.

—Theodore Roosevelt

The colleges and universities in which we currently reside have scarce organizational resemblance to their ancestral institutions at the turn of the century. At the dawn of the 20th century, a president and a handful of his advisers organized the range and scope of the institution's work. Faculty, loosely organized in departments or colleges, had neither tenure nor much of a voice in the leadership and direction of the institution. A distinct minority of the professorate conducted research of any kind, and the vast majority espoused no interest whatsoever in scholarly research pursuits, instead spending their lives teaching their young recruits.

Students were primarily from what has been thought of as the "traditional" college age of 18 to 22; part-timers, adults, the physically challenged, and students of color were more aberrations than accepted members of mainstream campuses. Except for a few campuses, white men taught white men. Although women students existed on campus, their course work was circumscribed by their gender, so we experienced females in home economics classes, but rarely in engineering, in nursing rather than in medicine, and mostly in normal schools that trained them to be teachers rather than administrators.

At the close of this century, we discover some areas in which academe has not changed. In general, teachers still stand in front of classrooms and lecture to a roomful of students. Class structures are remarkably similar;

they last for a quarter or a semester, and classes meet one, two, or three times a week. Students take courses to accumulate credits; when they garner the successful number, usually in 4 or 5 years' time, they graduate. Faculty assess student work by assigning letter grades as judgments of a student's mastery of the course material.

However, many organizational issues remain unresolved. Faculty still argue with one another over issues such as general education require-ments, and they are ultimately unable to decide what constitutes a well-rounded curriculum or an educated citizen. Administrators still apply business principles first utilized a century ago. The public still looks askance at the goings-on discovered on the college campus. Reports continue to be issued that point out the terrible decline in which academia finds itself. Faculty are suspicious of administrators; administrators are frustrated with the faculty. Parking is still in short supply.

Except for parking, I focus on these issues in this book. My overall intent is singular: how might we create institutions that are more respon-sive to the needs of our constituencies? We surely have had enough reports telling us what we do wrong and prescribing panaceas that amount to academic New Jerusalems; wonderful ideas, but unreachable except for the chosen few. I will argue here, however, that we are at a moment in academe that demands extraordinary organizational changes; attainable, doable, and necessary. Rather than accretionary change that takes place haphazardly, we need systemic organizational change that reinvents how we structure academic work so that we are more responsive to the needs of society. As James Duderstadt has observed, what we need is a shift to "learner-centered organizations that will characterize the 21st century, joining other social institutions in both the public and private sectors in the recognition that we simply must become more focused on those whom we serve" (Duderstadt, 1997, p. 7). The assumption that colleges and universities need dramatic organizational transformation is based on four views of the academic universe.

Viewing Academe

1. The Unbearable Shortfall of Resources

Many will argue that expenditures and revenues in academe have gone in opposite directions during the last 20 years; others may quarrel with such a generalization, but they concede that academe is less fiscally healthy today than a generation ago. As a recent report from Rand has summarized, "The United States has been under funding higher education since the mid-1970s" (1997, p. 10). The cost of instruction, for example, has risen 30%. As Michael Mumper notes, "With the sole exception of spending on libraries, there were substantial increases in every spending category at both public and private colleges" (1995). As with any institutional budget, there are costs that could be trimmed; yet, the vast majority of college costs are quite understandable.

The faculty as a group aged during the 1980s, and their salaries were collectively higher. Health benefits and social security taxes have been the fastest growing institutional expense, and these costs cannot be tightly controlled by fiscal planning. Regardless of what one believes about the humanities, the shift in majors away from the liberal arts and toward engineering, computer science, and other such concentrations has forced institutions to offer courses of instruction that cost more than the majority of college majors of a generation ago.

Expenditures for student services increased by 48% at public institutions and by 78% at private institutions between 1975 and 1990. There are those who might argue that such costs reflect a bloated budget in dire need of reform. Most of these costs, however, reflect institutional attempts to keep pace with the changing needs of society (Francis, 1990; Hauptman, 1990). Career placement, day care, admissions and financial aid, support for the disabled, computer labs, and a plethora of other services and programs are responses to the changing demographics, legal requirements, and expectations of society. Again, although polemicists have had a field day pointing to frivolous costs at particular institutions, the reality is actually quite different. In a competitive market, "customers" expect particular resources, such as child care, computer terminals, and so on, and if the college does not have them, then the consumers will take their money elsewhere.

As costs have risen, revenues have been unable to keep pace. As institutions raised their tuition to balance their budgets, more students became less able to pay the costs of college; simultaneously, institutions assumed responsibility for student loans, grants, and scholarships to a degree that was unheard of only 20 years ago. Ironically, in an effort to garner more revenues, institutions raised their tuition, only to find that they needed to generate financial aid in an amount that was greater than the amount of all the federal grants combined (College Board, 1993).

The golden age of research has also ended. The exponential growth of federally funded research that academe experienced during and after World War II until the late 1960s is no longer available. As David Goodstein, the vice provost for research at the California Institute of Technology noted, "We stand now on the threshold of our new and future condition: the permanent era of constraint" (1994, p. B7). The federal government's new philosophy against activism in socially responsive ways, its inability to manage costs, the legislative lack of desire to raise taxes, and the absence of public backing suggests that, in the future, funding for research or postsecondary education will not be available at the level it has been in the past.

State-level funding, always episodic, has seen more downturns than upturns (Council for Aid to Education, 1997). Education has received a very low priority for investment of public funds in many states, and there is very little funding to provide even if education were a higher priority. State governments in general are less able and less willing to pay for public higher education in a manner akin to what took place throughout the 1970s. Between 1987 and 1992, state appropriations per full-time student fell 13% (Quinn, 1993, p. 51). In its heyday, for example, 15% of California's state budget went to fund the master plan for the community college, state university, and research university system. The state portion that goes to public higher education is approximately 12.5% of the budget. The result is larger classes, lower salaries, and deferred maintenance. Few, if any, will say that the system is performing better because of the cutbacks. Furthermore, the expectation is that the state will gain 200,000 more students over the next decade. If the state were to fund these students at levels equivalent to today's funding (and not during California's heyday), then 20% of the budget would be consumed by public higher education. No one makes such a prediction. The result seems to be a choice between lowering quality and allowing fewer individuals to earn a college degree.

We arrive, then, with a troubling picture. The costs of postsecondary institutions have risen more rapidly than at any other time in this century, and revenues generated have been barely enough to pay for expenditures, much less to provide new outlays to keep pace with changing societal and consumer desires and needs. If anything, revenue income has become more complex, as institutions create off-campus businesses, entrepreneurial ventures, and development offices to undertake capital campaigns and fund-raising drives that will pay, not for prestigious items such as endowed chairs, but for basic services such as the upgrading of outmoded facilities. The study by Rand on the fiscal crisis in higher education estimates that, if nothing changes and academe continues on the same road that it is on today, within a generation "the higher education sector will face a funding shortfall of about $38 billion—almost a quarter of what it will need" (1997, p. 14). Such facts, however sobering, point out the need for dramatic change. The status quo will not hold. Is there a different way to do what colleges and universities do now in a more efficient manner?

2. It's Off to Work We Go

Who should go to college and what they should study have been twin concerns throughout the 20th century. Certainly part of the problem in answering these questions concerns forces external to the organization: what society needs from its workforce, and what the future portends for the workplace.

The 21st-Century Workforce

Whereas equity and access once were cornerstones of academe, there is no longer widespread support for such a belief. The language of academic excellence has supplanted a discourse concerned about open access to postsecondary education. Indeed, affirmative action is under significant attack, and the desire to upgrade the skills of those less prepared for college is less a priority today than a generation ago. The assumption of many of those who do not support affirmative action and other like-minded policies is that excellence and access are contradictory ideas. Consequently, authors such as Allan Bloom argued that eroding standards in higher education were the result of academe having been "saturated with the backflow of society's problems" (1987, p. 18). The "backflow" referred to groups previously excluded from college campuses, such as African Americans, Hispanics, and Native Americans. The result is that minority enrollment throughout the 1980s and 1990s at the worst times decreased, and at best has made minimal advancements (Francis, 1990 p. 37; Tierney, 1997). As college has become less affordable, more low-income students have been unable to complete a four-year degree and/or are unable to take out huge loans to pay for a college education.

At the same time, we know from labor department studies that, in 1979, a male college graduate earned 49% more than a male with only a high school degree. Today, that gap has grown to over 83% (Risen, 1994, p. A27). As Robert Reich has noted, "At every level of education and training, the pattern holds: The higher the skill level the higher the earnings, and the gap has been growing" (Risen, 1994, p. A27). We also know, for example, that four-fifths of central-city African American men with less than 12 years of schooling had jobs in 1968 to 1970; today that figure for the same group is less than 50%. We are faced with the stark reality about the last 15 years: While the participation gap between upper- and lower-income students has expanded, the focus of government support has shifted away from the poorest sectors of the economy to middle- and upper-income students. The result is that the goal of universal access to higher education is further away in the mid-1990s than it has been in more than a decade.

The 21st-Century Workplace

Debates during the past decade about what students should learn frequently have focused on the *canon*—a body of knowledge that everyone should know—and multiculturalism, and repeatedly have overlooked the changing nature of work and the economy. Discussions about the content of a curriculum often neglect pedagogical issues about how we teach and whom we teach. Yet, we have some idea about what skills are necessary for the workplace of the future. Analysts of the labor market are in general agreement that three forms of work are emerging in a global economy: (1) routine production, (2) service, and (3) symbolic analysis. These categories of work currently cover three out of four jobs in the U.S. economy (Reich, 1992, p. 180), and the skills needed for them will dramatically change.

We know that assembly line jobs and routine production work will become a vestige of the past in the 21st century. Economists anticipate that the country will lose 10 to 15 million manufacturing jobs over the next decade to foreign competition. New York City is an instructive example; the city gained 300,000 jobs in the 1980s, but lost 160,000 manufacturing jobs. The trend will only accelerate. Large factories that once employed thousands of routine producers can now be run by a handful of skilled technicians. The construction of an automobile took over 30 hours to complete a decade ago; it now takes fewer than 10 hours. Production no longer occurs in one plant in one city but throughout the world. Tires are made in Thailand, the motor is made in Japan, the body is assembled in Tennessee, and the car is sold in Europe. Such changes do not augur well for what we have come to think of as traditional blue-collar work.

Similarly, what economists have called "service jobs" will continue, but the nature of the work will change. Restaurants will still need waiters and waitresses to serve customers, but we also will have a large cadre of individuals who will telecommute from their homes and communities in ways unheard of a generation ago. Software engineers, video salespeople, e-mail servers, and small businesses are the kinds of new employment found in the service category. Such individuals will need specific skills to meet the needs of a technological society.

Those individuals who are "symbolic analysts" or knowledge workers will have increased importance in a global economy. Symbolic analysts identify and solve problems by the manipulation of images. Critical thinking, abstraction, innovation, and collaboration highlight the kind of work done by symbolic analysts. The symbolic analyst has learned to function in a digital and multicultural world. Rather than isolating himself or herself in a community of like-minded individuals, the symbolic analyst seeks to understand how difference operates in any number of forums; culturally, logically, and economically. The computer software industry in Silicon Valley is one example of symbolic analysts at work. Innovation, rather than the maintenance of the status quo, is highlighted. Teamwork is the manner in which tasks get done. And because the team is bent on experimentation, the focus of work by definition deals with abstract concepts and a form of thinking that seeks not merely to accept reality, but to change it and reinterpret it. The goal is to create new realities that generate new markets and ideas for capital formation.

The result is that a postsecondary education will be of increasing importance. Those individuals who do not get some form of postsecondary education will find themselves less economically advantaged than their peers from a generation ago. Colleges and universities also will need to transform what they teach and how they teach in order to meet the needs of a dramatically reconfigured workplace. Rote learning by students or redundant lectures by professors will be insufficient training for gainful employment in a global economy.

My emphasis here on *postsecondary* is purposeful. Certainly not every individual needs a bachelor's degree; however, it is increasingly clear that a high school diploma as currently configured is an insufficient educational credential for the workforce of today and tomorrow. Such an assumption implies that colleges and universities need to rethink how they function, and in particular, how they interface with other educational and business organizations such as schools, businesses, think tanks, and foundations. Rather than assuming a stance of disengagement from society, we must become more responsive. It seems foolhardy to prepare significant numbers of students in majors that offer no career opportunities; it is equally foolish to educate students for narrow vocational skills when we know that the nature of work is undergoing dramatic changes. For example, we must question whether every college and university needs a physics department if the graduates of the department are unable to find gainful employment. The question pertains to degrees that prepare individuals for one specific occupation that may be *hot* today, but when that area turns cold tomorrow or the next day, the workers will be unemployed. The answers to such questions are not simple. As I will elaborate in later chapters, if the mission of the organization is in some way tied to a particular area of interest, then a case may well be made for a particular department or area of inquiry. The important point, however, is that questions must be raised in a manner with which academic minds have not been comfortable. Postsecondary organizations need to be more adept at asking themselves difficult questions and forging relationships with new constituencies if they are to survive and play a critical role in the 21st century.

Academe is not a miracle cure. Colleges and universities exist in society and within an economic structure. Mundane work and low-income employment will always be needed in an economic structure based on capitalism (Mishel & Bernstein, 1994; Noble, 1994). Part-time work and dead-end jobs are most certainly part of the consequences of an economy focused on profit for the few over the many. The widening gap between rich and poor is not merely a gap between those who have a college education and those who do not. However, no one would advise an individual that a college or a postsecondary education is worthless; it is equally mistaken to think that a well-educated workforce will not be more productive for the economic and social well-being of the country in the 21st century.

3. Lost in Cyberspace

I began my doctorate at Stanford University in 1980. For some reason or another, I have saved a few of my term papers from that first year. When I recently glanced at the papers, what struck me was not the fancy academic jargon I used as a new doctoral candidate, but the manner in which the text had been composed: namely, on an electronic typewriter. I saw where I had "whited out" a misspelling or two, and how the professor had cribbed in a few comments in the margins. Four years later, when I began my dissertation, I had a computer, but it was hooked into the mainframe on campus; one disastrous afternoon I remember only too well absent-mindedly deleting Chapter 4.

The 1980s certainly do not seem like a distant epoch, but my examples are commonplace for those of us who work in academe. Computers, faxes, e-mail, voice mail, teleconferences, and virtual reality all have changed the way academics work in less than a generation. At no other time in the 20th century have we seen such rapid and far-reaching technological changes for the broad mass of administrators and professorate.

I now receive about 50 electronic messages a day; at the start of the decade I was not certain how to "log on," or even if it was necessary. The program I teach in has a web page, as does the Center. We advertise conferences via listservers. We increasingly tend to think of colleagues who do not use e-mail as troglodytes—artifacts of a past generation—when the broad use of e-mail has taken place only in the past decade. I now receive communication for meetings on e-mail, and frequently when we cannot meet in person, we will hold a virtual meeting somewhere in cyberspace. Every class I teach makes use of interactive communication that goes well beyond the formal classroom setting.

Technology is dramatically changing the way we work with one another, both within our organizations and with other organizations. I certainly am not suggesting that face-to-face communication is an artifact of the past; if anything, I shall suggest it is more important now than ever. But the technology with which we interact changes the scope and parameters of communication. Information in a technologically driven college or university is different from previous top-down administrations, in which boards of trustees, presidents, and their cabinets were able to explain issues because they controlled what was known. Such control is much harder in an age when an organization's participants all can receive the same news within a matter of minutes. Similarly, if what I noted in the previous section about the need for increased postsecondary education is true, then the potential for greater communication across organizations and units is possible, not a dream.

My point here is not simply that colleges and universities need to update their technologies, or that certain academic units such as libraries need to be dramatically reconfigured in a matter of years. Rather, my focus is on the sea change that we have experienced in communication technology and what the implications are for how we work with one another. The day has passed when simple truths such as "management by walking around" will suffice for what we mean by good, or even adequate, communication.

4. The Oxymoron: Academic Community

Tough times typically necessitate that individuals and groups come together; academe's current experience is the opposite. The tenure of college presidents is shorter today than it has been at any time this century. The relationship between faculty and administrators, frequently tenuous, appears almost stretched to the breaking point. Faculty morale often seems to have taken a similarly negative turn. Reports (e.g., Boyer, 1990, p. 75) continue to document the lack of community and collegiality on our campuses.

The disintegration of community, at least in its traditional manifestation, is not necessarily negative. Of course, we do not want to re-create a community in which women are treated as second-class citizens, ethnic and racial groups are excluded from entry, those in wheelchairs cannot make it up the steps to the first floor, and lesbian and gay individuals can lose their jobs simply because of their sexual orientation. The opening of the academic door, the inclusion of greater diversity, has created a fuller, more diverse academic community. And yet we must recognize that diversity necessitates structures that enhance communication so that we are able to understand one another, develop a communal ethos, and work in concert.

In general, colleges and universities have the opposite kind of structures. The faculty are housed in insular disciplinary structures that exacerbate, rather than stimulate, the ability to communicate across differences. A paradox exists in that, at a time of increasing interdisciplinarity, for the most part we work in structures and study ideas that decrease collegial bonds and understandings. A competitive ethic has taken hold in the academy where our structures reward individual effort and group efforts appear problematic.

Nevertheless, difficult times demand action and decisions. We need the ability to come together, to build a strategic vision of the enterprise, and then set about enacting it. However difficult change may be, the status quo is simply unacceptable. Organizations of tomorrow that are maintained in ways in which we operate today will become irrelevant to the needs of society. Fewer available resources, the radical change in the nature of employment, and the communication revolution all point to dramatically different organizational environments.

If what I have outlined is true, then more, rather than fewer, people will need postsecondary training. We are heading, however, to a time when fewer people will be able to afford such an education. Colleges and universities will become less rather than more diverse. Faculty will search for research dollars that no longer exist, and students will be trained for jobs of the past rather than the future.

The point here is neither to be a prophet of doom nor to suggest that change is impossible. Neither should we engage in apocalyptic finger-pointing. Academe's problems do not in general lie with individuals, but with the interrelated structures in which we find ourselves. We recognize that problems exist, but we have yet to enact a plan of action about how to deal with these problems as an academic community bounded by a common purpose that is socially responsive. Over the past decade, organizational changes have been around the edges of higher education's communities rather than at the heart. We have made stopgap decisions rather than strategic ones.

Michael Katz (1987) has written that the ideal community

> should be a community of persons united by collective understandings, by common and communal goals, by bonds of reciprocal obligation, and by a flow of sentiment which makes the preservation of the community an object of desire, not merely a matter of prudence

or a command of duty. Community implies a form of social obligation governed by principles different from those operative in the market- place and the state. (1987, p. 179)

Community, then, is framed by philosophical principles from which we then create plans of action. If we are to build a high performance organization for the 21st century, what might be these principles? If we commit ourselves to the ideals of what we believe academic life is about, but with an awareness of present context, then five principles frame how we will go about building a socially respon- sive campus.

The Commitments

1. Commitment to an Educational Community

Because I will write a good deal about the importance of increasing our organizational effectiveness and efficiency, and I will borrow ideas and concepts from the business world, it behooves me to point out the centrality I place on the kind of environment in which we work. We are neither simply a business nor an independent collection of individuals. To be sure, fiscal shortfalls and faulty planning can bankrupt a college or university. Individuals and units are also capable, if not actively encour- aged, of doing independent work in the kind of decentralized environment to be discussed here.

However, the university's mission is different from that of a company whose sole purpose is to develop a good product and turn a profit. In a postsecondary institution, we come together to help educate students and one another. We aim to help students gain some insight into how they understand the world for themselves. Our purpose is not to sell an idea, market a product, or inculcate individuals with a particular worldview. We aim to equip students with the intellectual and technical skills necessary to function effectively in a democracy. The manner in which we conduct these tasks is primarily by teaching individuals and conducting research; many would argue that there is no possible standardized way to proceed with activities such as teaching and research.

Even at a time when we are going through dramatic technological changes, education takes place within a community devoted to the ideal of empowering individuals. Education is more than a one-to-one correspondence between initiate and teacher. The academic community comes together to provide the intellectual space for individuals to consider issues greater than themselves. Yes, we must be more focused and develop greater cohesion than presently exists in academe. However, the struggle over ideas of what constitutes right and wrong, what it means to be an educated citizen, and what our role is in a democracy raises issues that by their very nature must be discussed and debated in community with others. To develop answers in isolation is to create false responses to communal challenges.

2. Commitment to Academic Freedom

If community is the overriding organizational structure of a college or university, then academic freedom is the overarching belief of the community. There have been many misunderstandings about academic freedom. In some ways academic freedom is easier to define by what it is not. It is not a license for a professor to do whatever he or she wants; it is not a belief that allows a physics professor to argue for a political viewpoint that is entirely unrelated to physics in his or her classroom; neither is it an idea that subscribes to political correctness nor bends to the whims of time.

Academic freedom, like the First Amendment, is also not something that every professor on every campus will test or call upon every time he or she enters a classroom or undertakes a research project. Indeed, many individuals will never explicitly call upon or need the structural protection for his or her academic freedom. But like the First Amendment, the infrequency with which academic freedom is invoked should not suggest that it is unnecessary or outmoded.

In a community that supports academic freedom, faculty have the right to substantial autonomy in the conduct of their work and the unfettered freedom of inquiry into different domains of thought, however unpopular such domains may be (Tierney & Bensimon, 1996). This right, this autonomy, does not mean that a professor may teach whatever he or she desires without benefit of peer review. Academic freedom does not mean that I can teach on Monday afternoons simply because I like Monday afternoon classes.

The obligation of the scholarly community is to assess its members to ensure that we are ever vigilant in upholding academic freedom, and also delineating what we mean by it. Assessment is done primarily through the tenure system, and this organizational structure has come under great debate, which I will discuss in Chapter 4. However, we ought not confuse structure with belief. Structures may need to change as contexts change. Our belief, however, ought to remain constant unless it has proven false. As the American Association of University Professors has noted, "Institutions of higher education are conducted for the common good and not to further the interest of either the individual teacher or the institution as a whole. The common good depends upon the free search for truth and its free exposition" (1985). No contextual changes have altered my belief that we must have as much a commitment today for academic freedom and the search for truth as we have had throughout this century.

3. Commitment to Access and Equity

Although the concept may be misunderstood, broad support always has existed for academic freedom. The same type of support can no longer be claimed for a commitment to access and equity in academe. Throughout the 20th century, public higher education has been seen as a central vehicle for increasing equity in society. Although the success of postsecondary education in this goal has been and will continue to be a subject for debate, one point that once united a broad fabric of policymakers, legislators, and the general citizenry has been the belief that a postsecondary degree is a path to opportunity for all individuals, not merely the chosen few from the upper classes.

Certainly one goal of the Morrill Act of 1862, which provided federal assistance for the creation of public state colleges, is an example of the belief that a postsecondary education should be open to all classes. The false deflation of college tuition in public higher education is intended to enable all individuals the ability to attend college. The GI Bill offered assistance to many individuals who otherwise would never have contemplated going to college. A public policy that did not care about access would raise tuition to the true costs associated with attendance and would not provide any loans or grants to students who need such resources to attend college. In large part, the decision to extend benefits and the possibility of attendance in college to the broad public has been based on the idea that all individuals deserve an equal opportunity. Such an ideal is a foundation of democracy.

In the recent past, however, many have questioned whether individuals ought to have a *right* to attend college and whether postsecondary institutions can provide adequate services to the population. And yet, if what I argued in the first part of this chapter is correct, we will need more, not fewer, well-educated citizens to participate in a global economy. We cannot afford a public policy that seeks to return to exclusionary times, one which differentiates between the haves and have-nots. As we close the 20th century, we must renew our commitment to access and equity as a core goal of the academy.

4. Commitment to Excellence and Integrity

Concomitantly, we must expect excellence and integrity in everything we do. Some analysts of higher education suggest that because of our focus on equity, we have lowered standards. Others point to the tenure system as giving tenured faculty freedom from criticism or evaluation. Still others believe academe's inability to define and to measure quality is a major failing that must be fixed. What constitutes, the critics ask, a well-educated person?

Alternative responses point out that excellence is an elitist concept, or that those who criticize tenure seek to eliminate it, or that our obsession with measurement does a disservice to intellectual work that cannot be neatly standardized. In our drive to criticize the academy, we also overlook that in this century we have built a postsecondary educational system that is the best in the world. If our degrees are *products*, then we surely do a better job with our global consumers than virtually every other business in the United States. Foreigners, for example, do not buy our cars or computers with anything close to the market share we receive from foreign students who flock to our shores to purchase bachelor's and graduate degrees.

And yet, we ought to do a better job evaluating ourselves and our institutions; the purpose is not for marketing or ranking, but rather as a way to discern how we might do better. Furthermore, the commitment to equity does not impinge on our commitment to excellence. If anything, we must move forward with the expectation that we expect superb performance from everyone; to lower our expectations shortchanges and denigrates the other commitments I have outlined. And too, if we do not hold fast to the principle of integrity, then all else is for naught. To lack integrity erases any measure of excellence to which we aspire; for an organization to be excellent it personifies integrity.

5. Commitment to Inquiry

A commitment to an educational community and to academic freedom suggests that we will be accorded the protection and responsibility for a search for truth. A commitment to equity and excellence stresses that all individuals are welcome and that we expect high standards. Each of these commitments, however, does not charge us with an action.

By highlighting the need for a commitment to inquiry, I am suggesting that postsecondary organizations and their participants are involved in a dynamic enterprise in which the status quo ought not to be tolerated. Surely we do not throw out ideas simply because they are old. But as engaged intellectuals, we also are not wedded to previous ideas merely because "we have always done it that way." The preponderance of paradigm revolutions in science and intellectual thought took place in laboratories and faculty offices on college campuses in this century neither by happenstance nor coincidence. We have previously nurtured the environment for intellectual inquiry and change; we must continue to do so.

I have outlined four views of the current context in which we find ourselves and have laid out the scaffolding for the five principles that guide my thinking about the academy and help frame the text. I neither believe the suggestions I will propose are a cure-all for the ills that plague us nor see myself as an academic "Chicken Little" worried that the collegiate sky is falling. If anything, my life in the academy has left me as something of an idealist; we are able to do better and we are capable of improvement. It is possible to keep pace with the flux of social and cultural changes that swirl around us and maintain those five basic commitments. And yet, if our beliefs remain stable, our organizational forms will not.

I turn briefly to a thumbnail sketch of the text, and in doing so, suggest what these new forms portend for us as we strive for high performance.

The Learning Organization

Different organizational needs demand different structures and frameworks. An organization that thrives on repetitive action will have a structural form quite different from the organization in which work constantly changes. A fast-food outlet in which a finite set of employees cooks and serves from a standard inexpensive menu, for example, has different needs from a restaurant that changes its menu daily and caters to multiple clienteles over the course of the day. An organization that is built for or that requires change is different from one in which standardized processes and procedures create profit and success.

From what I have discussed previously, postsecondary organizations are now in a time that demands a change-oriented structure that focuses on responsiveness. We need to create an environment that rewards experimentation and engagement with society, rather than the maintenance of the status quo and a standoffish attitude. Such a climate is always difficult to create, but perhaps more so when the organization is populated by individuals whose particular expertise relates to the art and science of critique.

Faculty find flaws in arguments not merely to be argumentative, but because in part the search for truth involves the rigorous investigation of intellectual claims in a specific area. The problem, of course, is that organizational change and experimentation are not a science, and proposals for action are always fraught with contingencies and unknown events. Organizational redesign is not simply the identification of a problem and the scientific discovery of a solution. In a perceptive article by Chris Argyris titled "Teaching Smart People How to Learn" he succinctly points out how too often "smart people" assume that what they need to do is fix problems, to solve dilemmas. However, Argyris notes that what actually needs to occur in organizational life is that smart people:

> need to reflect critically on their own behavior, identify the ways they often inadvertently contribute to the organization's problems, and then change how they act. In particular, they must learn how the very way they go about defining and solving problems can be a source of problems in its own right. (1991, p. 100)

How, then, do we create what many would call a "learning organization" for a college or university where smart people are presumably everywhere?

In Chapter 1, I expand on what I mean by a learning organization by delineating what reengineering means and what the implications are for postsecondary institutions. I look specifically at the scaffolding of a learning organization and concentrate on emergent structures and processes. In effect, Chapter 1 offers a theory of high-performance colleges and universities that will be responsive to the needs of their multiple constituencies.

The second chapter considers how to lead such an organization. New organizations demand new working arrangements that are less hierarchical and centralized, and more horizontal and localized. Leadership is concerned less with the analysis of an individual's characteristics or traits, and more with process, teamwork, and demonstrable outcomes. Interpretation, rather than autocratic directives, becomes a key communicative skill. Bringing people together and enhancing their potential are other abilities that I discuss with regard to leadership. By leaders, I do not mean simply individuals who happens to be college or university presidents, but rather the multiple localized units where leadership and reengineering go hand in hand.

Chapter 3 deals with the twin concepts of organizational focus and evaluation. How should an organization's participants decide what to do? Once they have decided on a strategy, how do they evaluate its success? I emphasize here the pitfalls that decisionmakers face in developing long-term goals during a technological revolution, but argue nonetheless for the creation of such goals. A college or university that is unable to orchestrate coherent, consistent action, or a university that drops one strategic plan and picks up another on a whim, is an organization that defies redesign. I underscore the importance of organizational focus by pointing out how formative evaluation takes place to ensure constant analysis, continual reassessment, and constancy of purpose.

Concepts such as reengineering, leadership, and strategic focus have specific meanings in a postsecondary environment as well as in other organizations. Chapter 4 pertains specifically to colleges and universities. At no time during the 20th century have we read so much as in the last decade about the need for change with regard to faculty roles, responsibilities, and rewards. Virtually everyone suggests that dramatic changes are needed in the life of the faculty, although few agree about what those changes should be. A redesigned organization is one that will have a quite different faculty role and reward structure. I focus in this chapter on three ideas: (1) enlarging academic freedom, (2) rethinking the tripartite role of teaching, research, and service, and (3) delineating a proactive ongoing evaluation schema for faculty work. I should caution that I do not call for tenure's abolition; however, I urge us to reconsider what is meant by tenure. A redesigned organization ought to expand personal liberties and create the climate for organizational commitment. This chapter focuses on how to do that for faculty.

The penultimate chapter takes on the cultural implications of organizational redesign. Change of the kind argued for here is not a simple process driven down a clear path. Accordingly, change agents need to rely on five properties; communication, incentives, power and control, information, and strategy in new ways. We have long thought, for example, that "strategic planning" is a necessary ingredient for change; what I will discuss in Chapter 5, however, is the pitfall of reform if we hold on to old concepts rather than invent new ones.

In the concluding chapter, I return to the ideas outlined here and consider what postsecondary institutions might look like in the next millennium. I highlight how we will have different organizations from what we have today and I summarize the guiding principles we might use to start on the path to reengineering.

The research for this book has derived from ethnographies, case studies, and interviews that I have conducted over the last decade and a half. What I attempt here is to summarize my work with the goal of offering practical thoughts about how to engage in organizational redesign. In doing so, I run the risk of offering solutions that may appear to be causal, when they are not. That is, I have outlined problems that exist, but my solutions are not causal—"if x is the problem, then you do y." I have tried to point out, implicitly based on my previous work, that x is a problem. If I can convince the reader of that point, I have then outlined how one might go about solving the problem if one buys into the notion of redesigning a campus for responsiveness and high performance. Certainly anyone involved in the rough and tumble of academic life knows that decontextualized rules of the road do not work, especially in the turbulent environment in which we now find ourselves. What we do need is a bit of reflection about the nature of our problems, and suggestions about how we might alter what we do. Thus, the book has been firmly grounded in theoretical assumptions about organizational life, and methodological frameworks involving qualitative research. I have tried to avoid presenting these backdrops within the text itself so that the reader might be better able to reflect on the argument presented and ponder whether the suggestions make sense for his or her own campus.

1

Organizational Redesign

The real voyage of discovery consists not in seeking new land-scapes, but in having new eyes.

—Marcel Proust

When I conduct case studies on organizational change in higher education, one of the questions I ask is, "If you were able to create a new institution, instead of changing the existing one you work in, what would be different?" Invariably, the changes that are suggested are dramatic: Eliminate departments, reconfigure the reward structure, rethink what tenure means, move away from static semesters, speed up the decision-making process, and have fewer committees. All of the good and dramatic ideas, however, are lost in my follow-up question, "Given that you do not work in a new organization, what kinds of changes are possible?" The second question is often met with long sighs, faces filled with frustration, and descriptions of organizational impotence and internecine power struggles.

Curiously, administrators and faculty, supposedly organizational rivals, frequently respond in similar fashion, albeit from slightly different perspectives. Both groups are able to raise interesting possibilities when asked about creating new organizations, and they usually sketch responses that cover the same landscape of departments, committee work, tenure, academic calendars, and bureaucracies. Often these groups blame one another. Faculty find fault with administrative blunders or a leader's inability to communicate. Administrators feel that the faculty role in governance stymies change and that faculty are too comfortable with the status quo to be open to experimentation and innovation.

An equally troubling comment is that individuals frequently feel that to maximize organizational efficiency, a sense of organizational community will be minimized. Presumably, if we have community we will be inefficient, and if we are efficient we will not be able to maintain community. The focus of this chapter is to point out how we might maximize a sense of community in these organizations by concentrating on how we undertake and accomplish our tasks. From this perspective, efficiency and community go hand in hand, rather than being contradictory or unrelated.

One of the chief complaints of faculty and administrators about the organization is the waste of time spent in committee meetings that accomplish nothing and the inability to develop and implement dramatic new plans. Efficiency in and of itself is a mindless, hollow goal. Similarly, the creation of community so that we trust one another but do not accomplish anything will lead us to fiscal, intellectual, and ultimately, spiritual ruin. I submit that we need high-performing academic communities. This chapter offers ideas about how to develop, nurture, and maintain such communities.

Too often I discover organizations where people's time, and eventually spirit, are consumed by mind-numbing tasks that have nothing to do with advancing student learning, undertaking innovative research, or being responsive to the needs of their constituencies. Instead, their days are littered with tasks that meet the bureaucratic needs of one constituency or another. For example, the provost wants all academic units to report how many advisees each faculty member has in a unique and new way that takes many hours in a week. A dean desires that all academic units rethink how they admit students and asks for a report. The faculty senate rewrites the faculty handbook and suggests that all departments determine what to do about grade inflation. An accreditation agency wants data collected about advising, and a state legislature requests that information be collected on post-tenure review. Taken separately, such concerns may seem valid, even helpful, and consume a minimum amount of time. However, what takes place all too frequently in academe are responses to such demands that delay an organization's participants from meeting the needs of their external constituencies and from strengthening a sense of community.

In what follows, I focus on four points of organizational redesign. I begin with a schema of what I mean by reengineering and then expand on its goals. I subsequently delineate the structural elements of the design, and conclude by suggesting good practices. My intent is to sketch here a portrait of how to create dramatic new academic communities and not be stymied by present constraints.

The Procedures of Reengineering as a Framework for Change

High Performance and Organizational Focus

Reengineering, a relatively new term in organizational literature, often provokes controversy and concern. Because some companies have reengineered and the result has been corporate downsizing, some individuals equate reengineering as little more than a clever ruse to fire employees. Others believe that organizations in general, and colleges and universities in particular, are much too protean for a structural analysis such as reengineering. Some have gone as far as to claim that it is little more than rewarmed Taylorism, a management tool for the 1990s.

Reengineering, stripped of the other ideas developed here, suggests that an individual or an elite team of individuals *builds* something. However, as noted earlier, the essence of building a high performance college or university revolves around the cocreation of ideas. Structure follows vision; it can not precede it. Therefore, what I intend to do here is not to offer an ardent defense of reengineering. Instead, I consider the procedures of reengineering that will be useful to employ in the redesign efforts of our colleges and universities as they become more responsive to the dilemmas that confront the broader society.

These procedures are important because academic organizations are frequently stuck or immobilized in the face of the crises that confront them. One reason for the immobilization is that they become bogged down by their academic dilemmas. A dilemma occurs when there are equally conclusive and unsatisfactory responses to a dilemma. For example, we want strong leadership at the top because we want positive actions to occur, and it may require strong leadership to get those things accomplished. We also want the benefits of decentralization since it is people closest to the problem or issue that are likely to make the best decisions. Similarly, we want everyone to be committed, but we also want individual independence. We do not like somebody else making the hard decisions, but we do not want to exercise the self-discipline that is necessary to make the decisions ourselves. Each alternative is somehow incomplete or unsatisfactory. There needs to be a way to bring the best elements or the alternatives together to resolve a dilemma and move forward and this is where using the procedures of reengineering is helpful. Reengineering is important because it will help an organization's participants get *unstuck* and move forward.

The idea of reengineering begins with a standard organizational premise: Goals need to be articulated for the organization's multiple constituencies and participants. However straightforward such a statement might appear to be, the idea is relatively unique for colleges and universities. In general, we either have eschewed goals or offered lofty language about educational excellence. The assumption of reengineering is that without clearly delineated goals, we will be unable to achieve high performance. What might such goals be for a college or a university?

As I will elaborate in the following section, an academic community geared toward responsiveness and high performance will have three interrelated goals that focus on (1) student learning, (2) faculty productivity, and (3) organizational performance. The organization's constituents are involved in the constant reflective analysis about what the outcomes for these goals mean. I touch on these three broad goals in order to demonstrate how a definition of high performance hinges on organizational focus.

Obviously, *student learning* will vary from institution to institution. How an institution defines student achievement will also vary. One college may measure student achievement based on relatively simple measures such as grade point averages or scores on examinations. Another institution may use the same criteria, but will have a different type of student and have different expectations. A third college may reject standardized measures and utilize a form of essay examinations or portfolio, and a fourth may monitor the kinds of jobs students get upon graduation to determine if the course work prepares people for employment.

Any of these criteria are viable determiners of student performance. What is not viable, however, is an organization's complete lack of criteria for analysis. Similarly, not only must an organization have criteria, but these criteria must also be shared and understood. High performance, as defined here, pertains to the widespread understanding and use of criteria for the analysis of student learning.

Faculty productivity is an equally critical component in a high performance college or university. Again, what an organization means by productivity will vary from institution to institution. Certainly, it should not be assumed that a productive faculty member at a large private university should be judged by the same criteria as his or her peers at a regional state college. One institution may feel that research is a very important element of a faculty job description and another may not. The challenge for participants in a high performance organization with regard to faculty productivity is twofold. On the one hand, since World War II, U.S. colleges and universities have rewarded research more than teaching, and naturally the organizational drift has been for faculty to focus on research. Participants in postsecondary institutions now need to redefine what is meant by faculty productivity, rather than accept national criteria that may suit some institutions but not others.

On the other hand, what we expect of one another is not adequately gauged. Tenure review is certainly a rigorous process and in need of change (Tierney & Bensimon, 1996), but post-tenure review is an area that demands even greater consideration and discussion. High performance does not mean that we create standardized criteria for an external authority whereby individuals are monitored and assessed as if we are widget makers in a production line. Rather, high performance gauges how individual creativity and talents might be effectively utilized to achieve the institution's mission.

Finally, we not only need to gauge how the student and faculty populations perform but also need an understanding of the overall *organization's performance*. Obviously, multiple activities occur in an organization that have no direct or immediate relationship to learning. If organizational processes are so confused that students feel frustrated by overly long registration lines, for example, or faculty feel exhausted by paperwork that consumes their day, then student and faculty productivity will be affected.

The leaders of an organization ought to be able to choose a handful of indicators that they use to gauge their progress. As previously mentioned, what the indicators are will vary from institution to institution, and they must be widely shared by the college community. The point is to develop criteria not for collegiate rankings or an accreditation body, but rather to create criteria that will help the organization's participants as an academic community to understand how they might improve and better serve their students and themselves.

This is easier said than done. Nonetheless, if we are to speak of high performance then we at least need to have an initial understanding of what we mean by the phrase or we will not be able to attempt to change. *High performance involves the processes we take to achieve agreed upon goals. It relates to the ongoing reflective analysis of student, faculty, and organizational productivity. Its measurement is not developed for external audiences or as a public relations gimmick; instead, we aim for high performance with our students, one another, and in our organizations, as a way to understand how we might mutually critique, support, and enhance each individual's work in the academic community.*

Using the Procedures of Reengineering

The procedure of reengineering is the engine that will drive high performance in colleges and universities. Reengineering helps an organization's participants rethink the academic organization. The procedures enable individuals and groups to challenge the status quo and its concomitant assumptions, practices, and structures so that the innovative redeployment of personnel and capital occurs and creates the conditions for a high performance organization. Reengineering means making implicit values explicit and challenging cherished notions of "how we do things around here." Dramatic change is based on a vision of what is to be achieved, thereby improving performance. It does not come by tinkering with systems that are already in place; it comes by fundamentally rethinking the enterprise and suggesting alternative notions not of what is, but of what might be. Those who employ such procedures are not incrementalists; they are visionaries with large goals and an appetite for significant improvements in student learning, faculty productivity, and organizational performance. Such a radical redesign raises three issues of what reengineering is not.

Reengineering is not total quality management (TQM). TQM seeks to improve the existing organizational structures and processes. The similarities between the approaches are that they focus on continuity and process. However, reengineering seeks dramatic change through comprehensive restructuring, not by improving what is already in place. Reengineering is also more than employing measures to increase efficiency; as used here reengineering is a means to increase high performance and community in academic organizations.

Reengineering does not overlook or destroy an organization's culture. However, reengineering does challenge a deterministic view of culture. The unacknowledged acquiescence to "norms" that maintain the status quo is questioned. Cultures are dynamic, not static, and too often we hear culture invoked when individuals do not want to change—"that's the way we've always done it here." We know, however, that traditional cultures are always in the process of re-creation or defining the future. Reengineering brings organizational culture into focus. Culture pertains to core values that arc cxplicit and supportcd by thc broad population. Culture also deals in symbols and "ways of doing things," but traditional cultures also remain viable and vibrant when cultural processes undergo dramatic reconfigurations by either current contexts or social forces.

Reengineering is a not a quick fix. Although colleges and universities that face significant challenges due to enrollmcnt drops or fiscal trouble may be more prone to turn to reengineering, it is not a cure-all that will immediately turn around the organization. Indeed, quick fix approaches in academe often have been notorious failures and insignificant fads. Because reengineering deals with cultural change, we ought not enter into the process by assuming that one merely needs to tinker, remove, or suture a particular wound and the problems that confront us will be solved. Instead, reengineering is a way of seeing and acting in the organizational world that is dramatically different today than yesterday. It will take time to reengineer the academy.

Since I have mentioned what reengineering is not, I will now outline the procedures of reengineering which are useful for our purposes here. Reengineering is a philosophy that employs five ways of thinking about the organization: (1) systems analysis, (2) innovation and experimentation, (3) permeable organizational structures, (4) cultural audits, and (5) shared knowledge and ideology. Consider these five points as a way of approaching organizational life. As I will elaborate, reengineers think of problems and issues in a comprehensive, rather than segmented, manner. Creativity and change instead of uniformity and stasis are sought, and fluidity, not structural rigidity, becomes the norm. We focus on symbols, metaphors, and communication as a way to build community and high performance. The mission of the organization is something that is widely shared internally, rather than used only as a marketing document.

Michael Hammer and James Champy (1993) helped coin the term *reengineering* for the business world. They define reengineering as "the fundamental rethinking and radical redesign of business processes to achieve dramatic improvements in critical contemporary measures of performance, such as cost, quality, service, and speed" (Hammer & Champy, 1993, p. 32). I entirely agree with their focus on "fundamental," "dramatic," "radical" change, and organizational "processes"; however, I am fully aware that academic organizations, for the most part, are not businesses organized around profit, but intellectual communities centered on the life of the mind and spirit. The manner in which those who work in academic organizations approach and solve topics and issues will be different. Although those in academe share common concerns with balancing budgets and responding to external constituencies, businesses try to maximize profits, while academic goals are broader. We certainly want fiscally healthy institutions, but as we reach for such stability we seek to be responsive, to maximize learning for students and faculty, to strengthen academic community, and indirectly, to contribute to the democratic sphere. The goals of fiscal health and learning productivity are not mutually exclusive, but they are more robust and protean than those of a for-profit company. The domains I have outlined may well pertain to businesses, but the manner in which I use them here relates to the postsecondary environment.

Systems Thinking

Problems are not approached in isolation, but rather in relation to other areas and issues of concern within the organization. We know that student learning, for example, occurs not only in classrooms, but also beyond the classroom with one's peers, in both formal and informal environments. How we approach prospective students and their families is no longer simply a matter for an admissions office; rather, it becomes a topic that cuts across organizational lines. We search for conduits that cut across structural entities.

Experimentation

Some organizations are set up to reproduce products and processes in an efficient manner, and it suits them well. McDonald's, the fast-food chain, comes to mind, where various employees move the product along a quasi-production line in an efficient manner to serve hamburgers to consumers. That kind of organization does not meet the needs of the dynamic environment in which academe currently finds itself. Instead, we need to build into the organization a desire to innovate and experiment. A risk-taking organization is one in which rewards and incentives exist for experimentation. Individuals need to know they will not be penalized for trying a different approach to a task; instead, they will be rewarded. Such an organization is a distinctly different kind of institution from those that seek to reproduce the status quo (Peters & Waterman, 1982). One implicit question that exists in a risk-taking organization is how we deal with failure. Not all experiments succeed, but we need to acknowledge that in a fertile environment some ideas will grow and flourish, so that the barren results of other projects are worth the risk.

Permeable Organizational Structures

The implementation of the procedures of reengineering leads to the reconfiguration of rigid lines of authority and decision making that ostensibly mark academic life. I write "ostensibly" because most of us acknowledge the lack of clarity that already exists in postsecondary institutions. Three faculty, for example, decide to create an interdisciplinary minor and spend the better part of two years passing the concept from their respective departments to a curriculum committee of their schools, to the executive council, and then to a college-wide committee that invariably has a subcommittee. The proposal is then finalized in a committee of the faculty senate and awaits the provost's final approval. Of course, at every step the idea is sent back to the authors for clarification and modification. Committee meetings are suspended in December because of the backlog of work that exists, and all activity ceases for the summer. By the time the proposal is approved, one of the initiators of the idea has left the institution for a better job, one has gone on sabbatical, and the third scurries around to recruit two individuals who have little interest in the idea but accept it for overload pay.

Is this parody or practice? Too many of us would say that it is standard practice. A reengineered organization is one in which such multiple, time-consuming levels of back and forth are streamlined not merely in the interest of efficiency but also because we trust one another's judgment and recognize that critical issues await us. Those closest to the actual implementation of the decision are given wide discretion and leeway to make decisions over how to control their lives and work. Obviously, checks and balances still exist, but the forced levels of decision making that have slowed down the process are voided.

Cultural Audits

An organization that utilizes the processes of reengineering is a reflective one. Both in formal and informal ways, individuals in the organization constantly need to reexamine their work and how it dovetails with the institutional vision. Summative evaluations used to prove or impress other schools or departments is not what I propose. On a macro level, I am suggesting that organizational units be involved in continual analysis about ways to improve what they are doing. The adage, "If it ain't broke, don't fix it" does not apply in the type of organization suggested here.

On a micro level, a cultural audit pertains to the ongoing assessment of the interpersonal dynamic and health of all areas and individuals. A brief argument that erupts one day for one reason or another may not be cause for grave concern; we all have bad days or minor disagreements. However, all too often, especially with faculty members who have high-strung personalities, problems fester and rigidify into an unwillingness to engage in constructive dialogue. Reengineering will not work if trust does not exist. A cultural audit keeps us on the lookout for ways to cement bonds of fellowship within and across units.

Shared Knowledge and Ideology

We constantly need to focus on what we are doing and why we are doing it. Reengineering involves the ability of all individuals to articulate their role in the enterprise and what the organization is attempting to do. People resist change because they fear that they will lose something, and because they cannot envision what the future entails. Certainly, not all ideas are valid, but the major problem that confronts academic organizations is not the lack of good ideas, but the inability to implement them. The point here is to get the organization moving, to enable us to get *unstuck* so we can implement the good ideas that develop. As I will elaborate in Chapter 2, one purpose of leadership is to instill in individuals a sense of direction and how their work will be valued.

We will then have the rudiments of the theory of reengineering and high performance in academe. The focus is on student learning, faculty productivity, and organizational performance. We must be able to articulate how we have improved in each area. We base the assessment on criteria developed on-site.

The assumptions with which we begin our work are in contrast to the assumptions of organizations built for maintaining the status quo. Rather than isolated thinking, we concentrate on systems analysis. Innovation, instead of replication, is encouraged and rewarded. Rigid and lethargic decision-making structures are replaced by fluid and permeable boundaries. The organization accentuates *reflection and process* over simple summative statements. The participants share in a mutually held vision of the organization where they are able to see and experience their role in creating change. What awaits us is how to elaborate on the goals we have espoused.

Articulating Goals

How can individual campuses know if they have achieved their goals? Put simply, we have taken the initial step toward high performance by acknowledging that goals ought to exist and defining what those goals are; the next step is to consider what we mean by each one.

If we cannot explain what we mean by each phrase, we run the risk of spending time on platitudes and semantics rather than achieving goals. Goals, missions, organizational purposes, and vision statements mean nothing and consume vast amounts of energy and time if an organization's participants are not able to articulate what such ideas mean. As Louis Pondy has noted, "The real power of Martin Luther King Jr. was not only that he had a dream, but that he could describe it, that it became public, and therefore accessible to millions of people" (Pondy, 1978, p. 20). Our task, however, is not to search for an individual with the heroic gifts of King, but to create the conditions where multiple constituencies within the organization are able to collectively develop a sense of organizational high performance. What, then, do we mean by student learning, faculty productivity, and organizational performance?

In what follows, I do not imply that these specific goals are to be applied to every institution, but rather I suggest ways to think about each goal so that we might be able to orchestrate constructive conversation on campus. As one administrator once commented to me, "I don't need to know what works; I need to know how to implement what works."

Student Learning

Three core activities frame how we think about the goal of student learning. First, we focus on an engaged classroom. The work of Chickering and Gamson (1987), for example, points out the elements of good teaching and learning (e.g., active learning and high expectations). Faculty and students become engaged in discussions about how broad ideas are defined, enacted, and assessed on their particular campus.

Second, we utilize portfolio assessment—the use of multiple indicators about what someone learns that incorporate standardized criteria with information specific to the individual and the institution. Students, parents, and the broad citizenry need assurance that students are learning in the classroom. Using standardized criteria is one approach, but other possibilities also exist that will be unique to specific campus cultures. Again, I am not suggesting that we mindlessly assign students grades or test scores so that the university might advertise how "excellent" they are to prospective admits or donors. A self-reflective organization is not merely faculty talking to faculty, or administrators talking to the public, but an engagement across groups about what we are and what we want to become. The portfolio entails an elaborated example of what the organization's participants believe to be essential to student learning.

Third, we concentrate on productive learning situations for a student that maximizes learning and minimizes the *downtime* and *drift* that too often characterize a student's academic career (Johnstone, 1996). The *classroom* of today is radically different from that of even a decade ago, much less a generation. Until recently the norm of instruction was a teacher lecturing to students in a classroom. Electronic technology and communication are changing that format. We must move beyond structural configurations that may have worked for an agrarian society but which are no longer viable in a postmodern world.

Each of these core activities is consistent with how I have defined reengineering. They afford ways to measure learning, but they also demand reflective dialogues across constituencies within an organization about what is meant by quality. Efficiency plays a crucial role, but we think of it as circumscribed by dialogues that deal with radical reformulations of academic careers rather than modifications of already existing structures.

From this perspective, questions such as the feasibility of year-round study or course sequencing outside of the semester or quarter system come into play. The pace of student learning might be both accelerated and individualized through technological advances. Credit hours might lose their viability in a culture where we acknowledge that students can learn what is expected of them in a rapid fashion. Learning becomes focused. Simple standardized measures of progress are no longer the only criteria upon which we base our judgment, and effective ongoing faculty-student relationships become paramount.

Faculty Productivity

We ought to have some form of understanding about our individual and collective goals for the next year and how we intend to reach them. Without such goals, our work becomes helter-skelter; a sense of unity and vision within a division in which a professor works becomes impossible; and the ability for the larger community to help the individual attain his or her goals becomes more difficult, if not impossible. We can no longer afford, either intellectually or fiscally, a loose confederation of individuals who do as they please and who have, at most, infrequent conversations about their own hopes and concerns for themselves and the organization. One way to frame how an individual intends to work and develop is with a performance contract.

As I discuss in Chapter 4, performance contracts should not be so rigid that they prevent faculty from capitalizing on unforeseen opportunities, but they should be firm enough so that the individual, his or her academic administrator, and his or her colleagues have markers upon which to base advice and judgement. In a community concerned with development and quality, there is an obligation to outline where we intend to go and how we plan to get there.

What an organization's participants can no longer sustain is the assumption that an individual is free to do whatever he or she desires regardless of organizational goals and needs. Again, the point is not to meet some bureaucratic formula about what an individual may or may not do, but to ensure that individuals meet the responsibilities and obligations they have to one another within the organization. The act of conferring tenure on someone, however rigorous a process it may be, ought not absolve either the community or the individual of a sense of duty to one another.

In many respects, the system we have developed for awarding tenure is akin to what has been pointed out as a flawed practice in the classroom. At the end of the term, we give final exams, and after the last student walks out of the classroom, we grade the tests or essays and assign letter grades. Such an activity is a bit like an autopsy; we have found the flaws and determined the cause of death. We are able to give a grade to our finding. Learning, however, is not only about grades. It is a continuous process that extends well beyond the artificial construct of a 15-week term. We now know that student learning is enhanced when individuals receive constant and prompt feedback.

At the end of 6 years, the tenure candidate receives a similar equivalent to such an autopsy. Some individuals are lucky and survive, and indeed thrive. Others discover that they have not succeeded. More often than not, no such learning activity will occur again with such rigor in an individual's career. A more coherent system will mirror what is encouraged of us in the classroom: ongoing formal and informal assessments that take into account individual initiative and potential. Rather than a retrospective pronouncement on how well a candidate performed over the past 6 years, we need prospective discussions about what the individual or all individuals, junior and senior faculty, intend to do, and how the unit will evaluate such plans. With such specific criteria in hand, we are better able to assess progress.

Organizational Performance

"Reengineering," write Bennis and Mische, "seeks to increase productivity by creating innovative and seamless processes that have an uninterrupted flow and occur in a natural order, with a natural velocity" (1996, p. 7). Flatter, cross-functional organizational units replace hierarchical systems that operate with centralized, top-down authority. Multiple layers of authority and responsibility are replaced by units that have the power to decide issues that directly affect them. The challenge, of course, is how the organization keeps track of decisions in a flat organization. As I discuss in succeeding chapters, tight, ongoing planning processes that have a direct relationship to the mission play a critical role. Without reports on progress that stipulate what a unit's actions are and how they relate to the overall framework of the organization, a college or university has the potential to become balkanized and fragmented.

We evaluate organizational performance not by microscopic changes, but by specified goals that have the potential for large, dramatic gains. For example, a target might be to increase learning by 25% or to raise admissions standards by a similar level over a specified time period. No longer can we hold on to fuzzy goals of "institutional excellence" or "increasing enrollment." Specific criteria that relate to the mission and goal of the organization drive action.

The mission and goal should be built on core values. Core values mean they are central or vital. As Collins and Porras (1994) have noted,

> If you articulate more than five or six, there's a good chance you're not getting down to only the core essentials. Ask about each one: If the circumstances changed and penalized us for holding this core value, would we still keep it? (p. 219)

Obviously, the strategies used to maximize productivity will change as the context and personnel change, but core values do not. A core value derives from the heart of our reason for being. It is not a marketing tool or public relations ploy, but rather a guide for who we are, how we define ourselves, and how we interact with one another. All else flows from the core. If we state that innovative teaching is a core ideological component, but we sanction people if their experiments fail, or reward research more than teaching, then we have an organization out of sync with its ideology. And if what we do is not a core value, then it can be changed, eliminated, or enhanced. No longer can we use culture as a way to stymie change. Rather, it is a way to define who we are, who we want to be, and how we measure our collective performance.

What, then, is an academic community that has utilized the procedures of reengineering? What would we hear if we stumbled upon one? In such a college or university I would expect to hear some of the following comments:

- I am part of a team; my work, however individualized, relates to the work of my unit.

- Students are our *raison d'être*; I focus wholeheartedly on creating an environment in which they can learn.

- Breathing, or living another year, is an insufficient reason for a monetary raise; I have a social obligation to explain what I intend to do and how I will get there.

- Yesterday's practices are not a sufficient guide for tomorrow; I am constantly rethinking the ways I teach, write, and work.

- Everyone counts; staff, faculty, and administrators are a team.

The goals of the organization orient activity. The framework for such a college or university enables us to think about action. If we accept that system thinking is important, or that structural permeability is to be sought after, what do we do? How do we move from a culture based on the status quo to one of change and innovation; how do we determine core values?

Structural Elements of Reengineering

Soft Projects and Ideological Maintenance

If we desire greater fluidity in the organization, then we need an organizational structure that enables quick, efficient decision making and implementation. At the same time, we also need an overarching philosophy that guides activity. Leslie and Fretwell (1996) have coined the term *simultaneous tracking* as a way to highlight the dual need for a clear core that enables decentralized action. Operational autonomy without a consistency of purpose leaves an organization vulnerable to losing its identity and culture. However, we have seen the risks an organization runs when it functions by way of a rigid, line maintenance structure. Such an organization can quickly become lethargic, incapable of responding to internal needs and external demands. How, then, might we create an organization that is fluid enough to respond to the press of the environment and, at the same time, cohesive enough to maintain a sense of ideology and group identity?

Line structures and soft structures can exist in relative harmony with one another where each has specific roles and responsibilities. Soft projects come and go and are reformulated according to specific needs; lines stay relatively stable. The idea of soft projects is most common in large research laboratories that seek significant sources of outside funding. The Jet Propulsion Laboratory at the California Institute of Technology is but one example of an organization that simultaneously has a line structure that remains in place regardless of outside funding, and a soft project structure that relies on outside funds. The two structures optimally work in concert with one another so that when funding is secured for a grant, personnel from a line structure might be deployed for the project. When the grant is finished, some personnel return to their lines, and others attend to other tasks.

Although we have commonly thought of a soft project structure as relevant for research outfits that attract outside funding, the concept might also be profitably deployed in redesigning academic organizations. I previously referred to the cumbersome decision-making process that paralyzes colleges and universities. The traditional structure of most schools has a standard line organization in which units and individuals report to other lines, other individuals. However collegial we might like to think our academic organizations are, we have in place quite typical hierarchical and competitive relationships, with departments and units seeking to expand their own influence and power, often to the detriment of other departments or units. A biology department chair argues her case more persuasively, or is a better politician than her geology counterpart, and a position promised to geology goes to biology. A student services unit assumes control over institutional research for no logical reason other than they saw an opportunity to increase their budget and no one stopped them. A president tries to recruit a vice president for a position that traditionally has reported to the provost, but the candidate says he will not come unless he can report to the president. All of us have similar examples that apply no internal logic to how decisions or actions occur; they are instead the result of the structures we have built.

Such political machinations are not inherently bad if the organization improves as a result of them. Indeed, the structure we have inherited in higher education has helped sustain academic organizations throughout this century to the point that we are second to none in the world. However, colleges and universities are susceptible to becoming outmoded due to the problems outlined in the introduction. We must concentrate on cost control and decreasing resources in an era defined by rapid technological, cultural, and communicative changes. In a dynamic environment that requires independent action among multiple constituencies rather than a culture of hierarchical dependency, we need to break the traditional organizational structure.

We, therefore, need to develop two organizational capabilities:

1. The ability of project staff to respond quickly, creatively, and effectively to immediate needs and problems.
2. The ability of line staff to focus on and develop long-term areas of excellence that undergo continuous improvement.

A soft project structure refers to the first theme, and line maintenance to the second. In some respects, we have always had soft projects. For example, I write a research proposal for a finite time period and hire a team of individuals for the duration of the project; when the project ends the individuals are not guaranteed any further employment. My use of the term *soft*, however, does not necessarily refer only to an externally funded project that employs people ad hoc. Indeed, that is not even the central concept. Rather, soft projects are those that arise out of need or opportunity, when groups of people from different academic arenas are assigned to work on a collective task that has a specified beginning and end point and may last a matter of weeks or years.

Teamwork and trust are fundamental components of soft projects; if personnel in soft projects are unable to effectively interface with line authorities in an atmosphere of mutual cooperation, then they will be unable to solve the mounting problems that confront them. At present, structure frames action by cordoning off discussion and creating internally driven grabs for power and authority. A soft project structure surely will not eliminate the individual drives for greater power; however, structural arrangements do play a role in how we cooperate and communicate with one another. In an age framed by the need for rapid responses to technological and communicative alterations in the larger society, we need to invent structural configurations that are not based on a centuries-old decision-making apparatus. A soft project structure is one such response.

Soft projects are much flatter than line organizations; they seek input from a wide group of constituencies rather than relying on a centralized team at the top of a decision-making pyramid. A secretary may well sit next to a full professor, a student, and a vice president as a coparticipant in a soft project concerned, for example, with enrollment management. Five faculty from differing ranks and disciplines may coordinate a curricular experiment in which the most junior professor is deferred to by her senior colleagues.

Optimally, a high performance organization has a staffing chart that is in constant flux and reorganization. Boundaries across departments and units become blurred, and colleagues move about in relation to issues, opportunities, and controversies that arise. How would it work? The following section is one scenario.

The mystery of dropping enrollment. A college has seen a 23% drop in enrollment and cannot pinpoint the reason. Multiple units are involved and each offers plausible answers as to why another unit has failed; central administration is often mentioned as a culprit. The admissions office claims faculty do not take an active role in recruiting; others claim that the department chairs and dean do not have a strategic plan to recruit individuals. Perhaps the recruiting documents are out of date, argue some faculty. Some believe the applicant pool is too small; others think the pool is fine, but not enough potential applicants actually enroll. The provost does not care what the problem is; he wants it solved.

Although the enrollment shortfall was predicted in the spring, and it became quite clear in August, it was not until November that the dean and her executive council considered any plans of action because they felt hard data were needed to make a decision. The registrar actually had a head count in September, but she was against releasing information that was not complete. Most faculty did not notice the significant drop-off in enrollment because the decline was widespread: two to three students per class. Due to the need to consult with various committees no actions occurred until February. The deficit they faced was now compounded by the second projected shortfall for the coming year. In effect, they were unable to rectify the problem for the current year, and their lack of action critically delayed any new plans for recruitment for the coming year.

A dean who believed in reengineering and a faculty and staff who bought into the idea would have acted in an entirely different manner. Some deans might have tried to bring together an inner circle of colleagues to deal with the problem, but soft projectization offers a more fundamental and far-reaching way to deal with an enrollment decline. We know that student recruitment is a multi-tiered process that involves various areas of an organization from a secretary who answers the phones to a faculty member who advises prospective students. We also know that enrollment declines are cumulative; unless a dramatic event occurred, such as an earthquake that destroys the campus, enrollment strategies are not one-time occurrences. They occur over a period of years. Time lags also exist. If we put in place an excellent recruitment strategy today, we will not experience the benefits for a year or two. If we develop an excellent brochure and mail it once, the result will be negligible; activities need to be systematically repeated.

Thus, the dean creates a soft project team composed of five to seven individuals such as one person from the student affairs office, one admissions officer, one professor, one division chair, one student, and the associate dean who chairs the meeting. They meet every week. They make decisions. They do not wait for perfect information, and they do not check with multiple layers of authorities to see if they may act. They simply act. The dean keeps the faculty and interested parties informed of what is happening on a weekly basis. Time frames, objectives, and goals are established. In this instance, the dean acts in her role of line maintenance to keep everyone in the organization informed; however, the members of the soft project have organizational autonomy. The project members stay together until they have seen two full cycles of new students and processes are in place; only then do line authorities to take over. In a crisis of this kind, a soft project acts as the central locus of change and command. Other areas of the organization necessarily need to respond to the project manager's directives, so that when the project recommends that no classes be taught with fewer than a dozen students, the directive is followed.

Such an example illustrates an emergency situation where active, visible change is needed. Although trust in any situation is necessary where shared governance exists and authority will be ceded to someone else, one might expect that in a moment of crisis management individuals may be more willing to cede power if they believe the project's participants act in good faith and are part of, rather than removed from, the community.

However, a soft project is not merely something to put in place when a problem overwhelms the organization.

Designing Curricula

The centerpiece of any organization is the curriculum it offers to students. We have used throughout this century the department (or division) as the central building block for curricular matters; many faculty would agree that it has become a stumbling block, rather than a building block. Creative approaches to curricular change are stymied as departmental fiefdoms develop that seek to protect turf, ensure student enrollments, and possibly increase faculty billets. Consider typical ways that faculty go about developing curricular offerings.

Sometime during the fall, the department secretary alerts the faculty of the need to submit what they want to teach for the following fall; the registrar, we are told, needs the information for the catalogue. Even though the courses will not be offered for 11 months, various levels of the organization need to check the curriculum for course scheduling, room assignments and editing. Individual professors dutifully consider what they are currently teaching and send in the same assignment that they currently use. Some individuals will be on sabbatical, so their courses are listed, but no instructor is assigned.

In effect, the curriculum exists by *rollover*; the next year is planned based on what is currently being done. A few individuals may experiment with a new course, or perhaps they may consider a new time to offer an old course. We probably could not invent a less consumer-conscious way to develop course offerings. In institutions that are tuition-driven it is particularly ironic that the person ostensibly in charge of scheduling is a departmental secretary.

Anyone who has entered into curricular debates knows that there are decided advantages to such a pattern. Most important, it avoids the pitched battles that occur when a department chair tries to get a professor to change a course offering. The secretary handles it. Hours of meetings do not take place, and the whole department relies on the wisdom that they should not try to fix anything if it is working. Such thinking, however, is contrary to the redesigned organization. The line authority of a division or department chair who accurately tries to predict course needs and times may be well-intentioned and moderately successful, but such actions will not produce dramatic changes.

We might think of departments as holding companies, but a soft project is where creative solutions can take place about curricular arrangements. One possibility might be that a soft project, rather than a chronological activity that takes place over a finite amount of time, is something that occurs in a 2-week period in the spring. During this 2-week period, faculty, staff, and students come together to build the curriculum for the coming year.

For such a project to occur, a different soft project needs to be created that investigates how to streamline the process, so that we no longer need a calendar year to project what we will offer. Lag time is a problem in accurately predicting and planning who will teach which courses. An individual gets a grant and will not need to teach what she had initially planned, but the substitute cannot teach the course on the days that are listed in the catalogue. A current event arises around which a faculty member could focus a course, but he has already committed to another course, so the "teachable moment" is lost. A third individual receives course evaluations back in the spring and decides to dramatically alter the title and course content so that it becomes an upper-level course rather than an introductory one. This change occurs too late because the course is in the catalogue. The individual must wait until next year, or actually 2 years from now. In an electronic age we should not need the same amount of time that was needed in 1960, but we do. A soft project's participants would pull in people throughout the organization to figure out how to streamline the process and enable curricular planning to occur in a subsequent project.

If this were possible, then the annual 2-week spring soft project would be a time when individuals come together to think about new courses to offer rather than simply to regurgitate what has been offered. If the culture is defined so that innovation and change are the norm, then faculty will enter meetings with the expectation that the status quo is insufficient.

Obviously, the problems of curricular change are not solved by the reformulation of work from lines to soft projects. However, we know the obstacles that have existed and continue to exacerbate our ability to develop interdisciplinary, timely, intellectual course offerings. The single greatest obstacle is not obstinate individuals or outmoded curricula; it is an organizational culture wedded to maintenance and the status quo rather than change. A soft project is one structural element that can help reorient the culture in a positive way so that people have the opportunity to experiment. In effect, we accelerate decision making on critical issues that demand expediency.

The obstacles to soft projects are not new, and they are entangled with one another. Fear, change, trust, and power go hand in hand in the creation of a culture oriented toward reengineering. All people, but faculty in particular, will resist efforts at change if they feel they are being bludgeoned or fooled. Because we work in organizations with shared governance, efforts to block ideas are more possible than in arenas in which the employees have no say.

Symbols and communication are the linchpins of success. An organization's participants who are asked to accept dramatic change because of fiscal problems will balk if they are not allowed to see for themselves the fiscal trouble, they do not trust their line managers, and the accouterments of growth continue to take place. A president who convinces his board to give him a raise based on his hard work retrenching the institution and who concurrently tells the rest of the college community that salary raises are frozen because of lack of money risks failure because of an action that many will see as duplicitous, if not unethical. Perhaps less unethical but just as problematic are related actions such as breaking ground for new buildings while the janitorial staff is laid off and faculty are told they must clean their own offices. Symbolic dissonance occurs when a department is told there is no money for hiring a replacement, but a new off-campus business is provided with significant start-up funds.

Generally, such examples provoke two responses. First, some individuals find it hard to believe that anyone would be so symbolically foolhardy as to give himself a raise or build a new office in hard times, although we have constant examples of exactly such action. Second, others will argue that such actions may be rationally justified. Some departments do need to be cut back due to fiscal problems, but that does not mean that all departments must be; raising the salary of the president so that he decides to stay at the institution if he is doing a good job may be a good move.

It may be a good rational move, but it most certainly is a horrible act if we want to create a culture aimed at reengineering. Most people will work toward individual and communal improvement if they are in a helpful, encouraging, and productive climate. Reengineering suggests that we need to focus on increasing organizational loyalty. People are not given marching orders or simply downsized out of jobs. The vast majority of us can buy into new visions of what our workplaces will look like if we can see ourselves in those workplaces and if we have a hand in building and profiting from our efforts.

One potential criticism of a soft project structure is that it has the potential to coalesce power into a few entities. An organizational matrix that is in constant flux without multiple levels and chains of command is ripe for abuses of power by a few individuals. An equally potentially damaging problem is that an organizational chart in constant flux runs the risk of destroying any sense of group cohesion or identity. If participants in soft projects are left to fend for themselves, they may make decisions that make internal sense to the project but have no relation to any overriding organizational goals. And finally, some individuals simply will not accept or support change. I do not accept a deterministic view of identity whereby we assume people cannot change. Some individuals, perhaps through personal background or current psychological makeup, will not accept the kind of dramatic efforts that are needed for organizational redesign and will resist change of any kind; but I believe such individuals are a minuscule percentage in an organization. We ought not tolerate behavior that obstinately seeks to force the brakes on any suggestion or new direction.

More critical, however, are the vast majority of people who recognize the need for change but are unsure how to proceed. The purpose of line maintenance is not merely a bureaucratic check to ensure overall coordination and tasks are accomplished. Instead, line units preserve the core ideology and offer individuals group identity and stability. The line unit ensures checks and balances. The power of the few does not supersede or pervade an organization that moves toward reengineering. Consider, then, 10 specific examples of good practice in an organization that hopes to employ the procedures of reengineering for high performance and one summative act of good practice.

Good practice communicates the need for change. Organizational change creates anxiety. Why change if it is not necessary? One role of organizational leaders is to communicate the need for change. The case needs to be made why change is not just a good thing, but essential if the organization is to survive and prosper.

Good practice operates on the assumption that people closest to the decision should normally make the decision. Those individuals who need to control processes or need a centralized chain of command will be lost in an organization that seeks to empower employees and flatten the structure. An organization that adheres to the procedures of reengineering assumes that those involved in the daily tasks that account for a particular task generally have critical insights about how to accomplish what they are doing. The challenge is to enable individuals to foster a sense that individuals will be rewarded for trying to improve, rather than maintaining the status quo. Too often, an organization's decision-makers implement rules that seek to prevent bad things from happening; in the redesigned organization the emphasis is on trying make good things happen.

Good practice articulates how decisions are made and follows the decision-making process. Individuals will be more willing to participate if they have a sense that they are involved in the decision-making process. They also need a clear understanding of how decisions are made and implemented. Cynicism occurs when procedures are not followed or individuals are overruled when a senior line manager disagrees with a decision. If we say we want people closest to the decision to make the decision, then we have to trust that those individuals will make the best decision. When they do not, we also have to trust the process. People make mistakes. Our faith lies in the belief that the structure we have put in place is the best possible way to achieve high performance over the long term.

Good practice focuses on constant improvement and recognizes perfection is illusory. I use the gerund *reengineering* rather than *reengineered* because organizations are never complete. Improvement is always possible and ongoing. There is no one best way to do something in an innovative organization. Risk assumes processes will not be perfect. True, the organization is not in constant *revolution*, but a vast difference exists in a college or university where the culture is geared toward enabling participants to seek better ways to perform and accomplish their work, and one that merely desires today's procedures and goals to be accomplished tomorrow.

Good practice fosters an argumentative, creative sense of loyalty. Loyalty is a tricky issue. We might confuse loyalty with a "bunker mentality" whereby dissent or disagreement is not allowed. But in a community of intellectuals, one fosters loyalty by honoring and listening to individuals opinions; to the extent that we are able to develop a creative tension, then an in-group sense of solidarity will be built that enhances overall productivity.

Good practice actively operates to nurture, develop, and articulate cultural values. An organization's culture is not something to be simply trotted out at office holiday parties or at graduation. In an organization that seeks to take risks, reengineer, and involve all of its members, individuals in the line unit must constantly communicate what the values of the organization are and how such values are demonstrable, viable, and personally rewarding.

Good practice utilizes dichotomous thinking. Immediate, specific, measurable goals are sought, and at the same time a sense of organizational identity is built that defies measurement. An organization's participants demand short-term performance and recognize that some activity will have long-term intangible benefits. We enable operational autonomy to exist at the same time that we seek mission-oriented control.

Good practice communicates the desire for change and rewards change efforts. A commitment to a dynamic culture must be built; it does not naturally come into existence. If an organization's participants want individuals to innovate and experiment then the organization must be willing to let individuals fail. The reward structure must provide adequate incentives to take creative risks.

Good practice encourages self-reflectivity and individual responsibility. Higher education professionals believe, however unfairly, that the assessment movement has fostered external evaluation. The response often has been to look at evaluation merely as more paperwork that needs to foil or placate external authorities. Good reengineering practice also assumes that assessment is critical, but it is done in a self-reflective manner that puts individual responsibility at a premium. Individuals involved in dialogical assessment are forward looking. They think about ways to improve and they assume that improvement can and will occur if the correct environment is developed.

Good practice reduces rules. Standards certainly exist, but in an organization that is risk-taking, individuals and participants in soft projects need a high degree of autonomy to make decisions. Empowerment, rather than a catchword, becomes central by focusing on the processes by which we provide people decision-making power and voice. The ability for members to have a voice in the organization pertains to enfranchisement, and the respect, tolerance, and nurturance of formerly disenfranchised players.

Good practice conveys high expectations and recognizes change occurs over time. A final, summative thought about reengineering and performance: Incremental changes are eschewed for substantive and significant goals. Change agents also recognize that reengineering is neither a stopgap nor an immediate undertaking. Radical process redesign begins immediately, but the successful implementation of these processes and the achievement of demonstrable, significant results takes time, patience, and leadership. We now turn to the elaboration of leadership.

2

The New Face of Leadership

You can't depend on your eyes when your imagination is out of focus.

—The Connecticut Yankee

Few topics have been more studied and discussed throughout this century than leadership. We usually have looked at leadership as being invested in one person, generally someone who is at the top of the organization. Leadership has had a distinctly positive ring to it. "He's not a leader" is as damning a comment to the same degree that "She's a natural leader" is a compliment. Although the language changes from time to time, we frequently think of traits, characteristics, or attributes that account for leadership. Good leaders are courageous, moral, willing to take risks, active listeners, excellent communicators, able to espouse a vision, and able to stimulate people. Bad leaders cannot do those things. Indeed, the idea of a *bad* leader is contradictory. We might have a bad baseball player who is a weak hitter, or a bad senator who is unethical, but almost by definition, leadership equates with success. A leader cannot be bad, for if he or she were bad we would not think of them as a leader. No wonder everyone wants to be a leader.

We have waffled about whether leadership can be learned or if it simply comes naturally. Since well before Thomas Carlyle's statement, "[the] history of what man has accomplished in this world . . . is at bottom the History of the Great Men" (1897, p. 1), many have believed that leaders are born, not made. Others have assumed that we can teach people how to be leaders. A friend once told me a book with leadership in the title is a sure seller, because individuals buy books that help them think about how to do their job better. Presumably, "Great Men" do not need books or "how to" manuals. Institutes, conferences, and personal trainers all focus on executive leadership training.

The contrary view has been that leadership does not exist in the late 20th-century organization. True, heroic figures, such as Mahatma Gandhi, Ida B. Wells, Martin Luther King, Jr., and Abraham Lincoln, come to mind and have always populated the universe, but organizational leadership is another matter altogether. Over the last generation, we have read tracts about organizations, especially colleges and universities, where leadership is said to be impossible and college presidents are "blind men on a freeway" (March & Cohen, 1974; Moore, 1971). Anyone who has studied the college presidency during a time of declining resources, a stagnant economy, and increased sociocultural problems might surely agree with the observation that leadership, either of great men or someone who learns the ropes, is nearly impossible.

The point of this chapter is neither to reject the idea that leadership is learned or inherited, nor to bemoan the inability of individuals to exert leadership. In a redesigned organization, leadership has a different meaning and intent from the overused either/or approaches outlined here. Leadership is not invested in an individual who single-handedly transforms the organization. Individuals can, however, help create, stimulate, and maintain the environment for change. In what follows, I first outline the new face of leadership and then consider the implications of leading by design. Along the way, I offer questions to consider for the reader's specific organization. The ability to answer these questions in a manner that is widely shared throughout the organization reveals in part the kind of leader the organization has and the type of college or university it will become.

Finally, when I write of leadership, I do not intend to imply that leaders reside only in a president's office. Indeed, as I noted earlier, organizational redesign depends upon leadership at various levels. True, a college president exerts leadership in a different context from a department chair, dean, or vice provost, but unless leadership is utilized throughout the organization, a college or university has little chance of successful redesign. As James Duderstadt (1997) has noted, "The abilities of universities to adapt successfully to the revolutionary challenges they face will depend a great deal on an institution's collective ability to learn and to continuously improve its core competencies" (p. 14). Accordingly, I submit that leadership needs to be exerted at multiple levels and in multiple manners, not merely by the person who temporarily inhabits the president's quarters.

Tangos

Implicitly, we have long known that leadership is multifaceted and multidimensional. One cannot lead alone. I am not a leader if no one else is involved. A man on a desert island or a lone woman on a life raft is not a leader. We might say they exhibited courage, stamina, a survival instinct, or heroism, but if the focus was on one individual's acts, then the word *leadership* would not enter our vocabulary. Similarly, when we say that someone is "one of the leading authors of her generation," or a "leading figure in the National Football League," we are not necessarily referring to leadership, but rather to prominence. A leading figure or author may or may not be a leader.

Leadership is a comparative, reciprocal process. We define leadership in context. We cannot have leaders without followers. Leadership is not simply the end result, but the processes we use, and the routes we take, to get where we are going. It takes two to tango; the same could be said about leadership.

Leadership in Cultural Context

We have talked about the culture of an organization for a generation, but we have yet to fully understand the implications for leadership. An initial, facile interpretation had administrators thinking that if they "managed by walking around" they were exhibiting cultural leadership. Another interpretation was that an organization's culture was like a faucet that could be turned off and on at appropriate moments. A speech on commencement day was an act of cultural leadership; developing the budget was not. Another assumption was that cultural leadership was a style; following it was the belief that all organizations had more or less similar cultures. I say "more or less" because we saw studies that tried to point out cultural types according to various criteria, for example, strong vs. weak; family-oriented vs. bureaucratic vs. political. Essentially, though, every culture was similar, or if a culture was very different, then it was an aberrant culture in need of repair.

Leadership exists within a cultural framework, and culture is not something that can be turned on and off. Think of how people learn about an organization's culture. They might comment on a president's speech, but more often than not when people talk about their organization's culture, it is generally about small, indirect actions. People note who sits with whom in the faculty club, whether meetings begin or end on time and how they are conducted, whether the president attends or avoids faculty senate meetings, and a host of other discrete events that take place in the daily life of any organization.

In *The Web of Leadership* (Tierney, 1988), I conducted an ethnography of leadership at a small, private college. The president frequently employed grand cultural acts such as speeches at the start of the school year and at commencement. I also observed actions in which individuals interacted on a daily basis in the mail room or the lunch room and the president never entered. These actions were cultural, albeit one of many small activities that take place during the course of any day. If one wants to make sense of the culture, we must investigate the contextual phenomena that exist in the interstices of organizational consciousness.

Although actions and organizations may exhibit similarities, we do not help the administrator by pointing him or her toward a typology of cultures to see where their organizations are because this would reduce leadership to a series of isolated acts and styles. People need a more nuanced approach to understanding culture. Certainly, similarities exist. Faculties exhibit common characteristics, and how one deals with them may differ very little whether we are at a small private university or a large public state college. A college president who skips the annual beginning of the year staff retreat has likely committed a cultural blunder regardless of the size or location of the institution. A dean of a small- or medium-sized school who does not learn the names of the faculty also has sent a message, whether the school is education, public administration, or nursing. And yet, cultures are unique. Leadership within culture must also be unique.

What, then, is organizational culture, and what are its implications for leadership? Why is cultural leadership so important in a book about organizational redesign? Culture pertains to the set of symbolic processes, ideologies, and sociohistorical contexts at work in an organization; it expresses identity through the daily workings of the organization's partici-pants, and it undergoes constant (re)interpretation.

Such a definition offers specific ways to think about cultural leader-ship. Rather than a manager who oversees organizational action, the leader becomes someone who interprets action and recognizes that each situation and context is unique. All organizational life is *up for grabs* with regard to how individuals envision their future.

At the same time, individuals operate within a distinct historical framework that helps define how work gets done. The import of such an approach with regard to organizational redesign is crucial insofar as times of change require constant interpretation. In an organization in which the status quo persists, processes, symbols, and rituals are reinterpreted, but they do not go through the sea change that might exist when dramatic new structures are put in place.

And yet, structure does not equate with culture. "That's the way we have always done things around here" ought not to be a suitable refrain with which to stymie progress. If such a phrase is true, then one might assume traditional cultures are monochromatic, static, and unchanging. The opposite is the case. Either through external necessity, as has been the case with Native American cultures on this continent, or through internal stimuli, as has been the case with nomadic tribes in the desert, change constantly surrounds traditional cultures, sometimes slow and lethargic and at other times abrupt and rapid.

Organizational redesign is dramatic and long-range. How the organi-zation's participants have done the work of the organization in the past will change and if success is to be achieved the transformation is not temporary or stopgap; it is fundamental. In a world in which all acts, structures, and events are construed as symbolic, it is essential to take into account the symbolic life of concrete phenomena. The leader needs to be able to develop the sense that changing structures do not destroy core beliefs. Structures change; core ideologies undergo contextual interpreta-tion but remain in place unless found to be false.

Follow the Leader

Individuals populate an organization's culture. Too often, we personify a culture as if it is an independent entity, a plant that we need to nurture or grow. Cultures do not exist independent of people. Leadership cannot exist without followers. As Kouzes and Posner (1993) have succinctly pointed out, "Strategies, tactics, skills, and practices are empty unless we understand the fundamental human aspirations that connect leaders and their constituents. If there is no underlying need for the relationship, then there is no need for leaders" (p. 1). The interrelationship among leader, culture, and individuals is inextricably woven together; they do not exist independent of one another. In some respects, the interrelationship of the three takes on increased importance, even urgency, as we approach the close of the 20th century.

Throughout the 20th century, Americans have experienced declining participation in social and familial groups that once seemed commonplace. Individuals who grew up in the 20th century prior to World War II frequently lived in large families. The families resided in one town, and individuals usually did not move or were not transferred in their jobs. People's stories about life "back then" are replete with discussions about religious groups, working-class baseball leagues, singing fraternities, and inner-city events and socials that seemed to consume most of their waking hours. Today, the academic's working hours are more likely to focus on work and home; frequently work consumes more time than even home. The numerous social groups of an earlier generation have evaporated. I intend here neither to bemoan that those days have past, nor to engender reasons why they have. I simply point out that they have.

The wonders of technology also have provided us with unforeseen opportunities which are at the same time risks. Faculty no longer feel compelled to go to the office every day, and they will work just as hard at home as at the office. They are connected to their offices via e-mail, phone, fax, and voice mail. A professor's mandatory attendance on campus has been reduced. Technology's wonder will only increase. The idea of how academics physically spend their academic lives may change dramatically in the future.

Similarly, in Chapter 1, I outlined how soft projects may be a parallel structure to the traditional, stand-alone structure of today; such structures, however fluid and necessary, also will alter traditional working relationships. Indeed, I offer concepts such as soft projects because they will revolutionize traditional working relationships. We also must be cognizant of the cultural ramifications of such actions and account for how an organization's participants will incorporate needed cultural and psychological dimensions in the reengineered college.

However much one may embrace technological change and innovative structures, the implications for individual and cultural interpretations are vast. Surely, the example pointed out at the outset about managers who walk around becomes irrelevant if no one is on campus. If how an individual learns about an institution is based on spending time in interactions and physical proximity to others in the culture, then such learning will be lost or reconfigured by electronic transmutations and constantly changing structural arrangements.

Herein lies an example of how structures need to change, but equally essential, beliefs need to remain. The use of e-mail instead of walking next door to chat with one's colleague does not suggest that the organization's culture is dead or that the individuals still do not have a need and desire to communicate with one another in ways more significant than a dozen lines on a computer screen. Indeed, the earlier suggestion that culture takes on increased importance lies with the realization that individuals exist in fewer, not more, social groups than in the past. The family as a social unit continues to erode. Smaller families, single-parent families, dual-career families, and mobile family members all point to groups who do not live the way individuals lived a century ago.

People also work more hours today than a generation ago. Whereas we once thought that individuals might have more leisure time and even a 4-day work week, instead we find that individuals have less leisure time and frequently work on weekends. These work habits are especially evident among tenure-line academics (Tierney & Bensimon, 1996).

The century began with social interaction that was multiple, commonplace, and ongoing; today it is increasingly singular, erratic, and uncommon. The work environment takes on increased importance. I am not a social psychologist or futurist, so I offer no observation whether such changes are good, necessary, or here to stay. However, it is important to recognize the consequences for individuals, an organization's culture, and its leadership.

As Kouzes and Posner (1993) pointed out, the reciprocity of leadership resides with the individual's needs. If social and organizational connections have lessened throughout the 20th century, then it stands to reason that the need for meaning only increases in those organizations that remain as the workplace. Individuals spend more time in one organization; whereas in the past, the workplace may have proven itself to be unimportant for some individuals or merely a way station en route to other social bonding activities. We now find that people's organizations are central rather than secondary. To compound the problem, technology changes the way individuals "interface" with one another. The copy editor for this book, for example, is someone with whom I speak and work a great deal, but have never met.

The importance of cultural leadership increases. I pointed out earlier that culture pertains to symbolic processes. Leaders play a fundamental role in explaining, interpreting, and creating the conditions for individuals to identify and bond with the organization and the culture. How is this done?

The Process of Leadership

Processes and goals do not contradict one another. I have often listened to "bottom-line" leaders deride a concern for process. I will hear, "Who cares about the process, if at the end of the day the bottom line doesn't show a profit?" Like so many arguments stated in that fashion, one cannot argue against it. When someone says, "I'm for efficiency," it is silly to say I am not. If a college president tells me her bottom line is a balanced budget, increased enrollments, and pay raises for everyone, then who am I to ask, "Did you take care of the process you used to get your bottom line?"

However, in academic organizations in general, and in ones that seek to utilize the procedures of reengineering in particular, we must attend to process and outcomes. Yes, there are organizations in the United States in which leaders have used the "meat cleaver approach" to restructuring and some kind of goal has been reached—increased profits, larger shareholder earnings, a better product. However, research findings show over and over again that attention to process stimulates the willingness to change and creates the climate for long-term, rather than temporary, changes.

Organizational redesign and a commitment to high performance focuses on long-term, systemic reform. Leaders, then, need to consider how the organization achieves "the bottom line" in a culture that will undergo significant change and that includes individuals who yearn for commitment and understanding of what the organization is and will be. The point is not simply to make people feel good, as if the process in which individuals involve themselves has no end point on which to measure their success. Academic work is not an intellectual fun house where leaders ask the participants to go along for the ride, try to make it as enjoyable as possible, and thank them for coming along at the trip's end.

Rather, the assumption here is that when leaders pay attention to process and create the conditions under which people are able to perform better, a twofold payoff occurs; the organization is more likely to reach their goals and people are more likely to feel good about themselves and the organization. Such an assumption stands in contradistinction to what I have called the meat cleaver approach, whereby we assume people need to be forced into better performance and goals occur regardless of process. I submit that most individuals in an organization, and in particular at this moment in American history, want to improve and want to help their organization improve. Inattention to culture, or a cynicism about individual behavior and motivation, cannot create the environment for organizational redesign. The task of leadership, then, is to interpret the internal and external environments to the members, create the ability for individuals to feel palpably toward the culture in which they reside, and to help set the processes that will be used to achieve significant goals. How?

Leadership Quiz 1

1. If someone unfamiliar with academe asked me what the culture of my institution was, what would I say?
2. What do individuals expect from the leader, and what do I as a leader want to change of those expectations?
3. What do people care about here?

Leadership by Design

The portrait of the singular leader who points in the direction that the organization will take, and by pure will moves the constituents in that direction, is at best a sketch of the past, and at worst a tragic mistake for colleges and universities of the future. In Peter Senge's (1990) work on learning organizations, paraphrasing Lao-Tzu, Senge points out the type of leadership needed today: "The great leader is he who the people say, 'We did it ourselves'" (p. 340). A leader who wishes to redesign a department, school, college, or university is someone, then, who has a deft touch and is capable of creating the conditions for the institution's participants to enact change, rather than assume that he or she can do it alone.

We have often used metaphors to convey our meaning of leadership. Leaders are generals, coaches, orchestra conductors, and ship captains. These words have tried to impart different meanings. A general is in charge of an army that wages war; the general's power is all-encompassing. The term *coach* sounds less militaristic and more dialogical, although some coaches are probably more comfortable being thought of as generals. An orchestra conductor has multiple individuals and groups to coordinate, and a ship's captain plots directions and is acutely conscious of the external environment.

Although these metaphors are distinctly different from one another, they also share remarkable similarities. Leadership is an individual act, and followers follow. The battle plan, game plan, symphony, or course has been set. A leader's role is to have his or her minions wage a winning war, play a successful game, entertain with the most melodious music, or sail the smoothest seas. In effect, the leader has the plans, and the followers' brilliance is in carrying them out. One may have to improvise along the way, but nonetheless when the organization begins its activities the assumption is that the leader has some form of project design.

The portrait is also of an active person, a *doer*, someone the organization cannot do without. An army bereft of a general will lose discipline and coordination. A team without a coach will be unable to develop a cohesive style rather than an individualistic one. A large orchestra without a conductor will produce cacophony, not symphony. A ship without a captain will float aimlessly, regardless of the plan.

What is wrong with these metaphors? A restructured organization needs leaders who are designers of protean structures capable of change and modification. The previous metaphors assume that a plan has been set and that the leader implements the plan. In many respects, the implicit assumption underlying the traditional views of leaders harkens back to the theoretical paradigm of positivism, which assumes that individuals can comprehend, coordinate, and manipulate reality. But in a world undergoing rapid technological and social change, it is foolhardy to believe an organization's participants can predict events as if they are waiting to happen. I discussed in this chapter how culture circumscribes organizational action. Therefore, the argument here is to think of organizational life within a cultural framework in which the participants are in a constant state of re-creation and interpretation. The leader's challenge is to design a malleable framework that enables people to work with one another toward high performance.

We have often chosen rigid leadership stances because we hope to manipulate reality; we fear that too much constituent authority, influence, and control will lead to organizational stasis or chaos. However, in the future rigidity will not enable rapid responses. If we do not trust individuals then we will remain trapped solving problems in an isolated, segmented fashion rather than in a systemic manner. In short, the view of a heroic leader whether a general, coach, conductor, or captain is fatally flawed for those colleges and universities that want to redesign themselves.

Leadership from this perspective is more team oriented than individualistic. True, a coach is part of a team; I am not suggesting the leader stands apart from the team. I also am not implying that a leader develops a plan or design in isolation and then descends from the mountaintop with strategies about how the organization is to proceed. Those leaders who are designers are much less directive and more facilitative. Design is comprehensive and systemic, not unitary or isolated. This view of leadership is one where individuals are encouraged to think about how the parts are interrelated. Too often we do the opposite; and we let different components of the organization progress or regress in isolation and have individuals work alone on their problems.

Two issues become crucial for the leader. The first is one of definition, the second concerns team enhancement and the development of soft projects. Leadership as design means that new plans are set in motion rather than those that already are in existence. An organization's participants are in a constant state of anticipation and interpretation instead of implementing a plan and sticking to it. The leader facilitates project accomplishment by nurturing effective and efficient teams.

Anticipatory Designs

I discussed in Chapter 1 the case of a college that faced an enrollment decline. Individuals and units worked in isolation from one another, so no sense of systemic thinking guided the organization. Although problems were anticipated prior to their actually happening, no one thought to be on the constant lookout for such problems in part because of the loose coupling that exists in academic organizations. The left hand all too frequently does not know what the right hand is doing. Instead, the problems were dealt with only after they occurred. In an age when society has realized that preventive medicine can lower health costs and keep people healthy so they do not get sick, I am suggesting that organizations also consider ways to put into play anticipatory designs so that colleges and universities stay healthy rather.

The leader's task is to put into play a design sketch that enables people to see beyond their own sphere and embrace working together to solve problems before they arise. The leader neither solves the problem nor necessarily defines the answers to the specific problem. Instead, the leader's challenge is to provide the structure, incentive, and decentralized authority to enable those with whom he or she works to deal with the issue. Such a role is much less grandiose than that of the orchestra conductor who accepts the applause at the end of the concert and decides the protocol for the order in which someone in the orchestra should stand and take a bow. In many respects, the leader who is a designer is off-stage. The sense of accomplishment is in seeing others do well.

I know of two colleges that faced identity crises. As small public institutions, they were unsure how to meet enrollments and reconfigure faculty roles. At one institution, a president came in, swept house, created significant short-term gains, and then left the institution for a better job; soon thereafter, the traditional problems of identity and faculty roles crept back in, although this time the school was in a more dire financial strait, so the problems were more significant.

At the second institution, the president arrived and set about speaking with every individual on campus, from vice presidents to the custodial staff, about the problems they saw and ways to improve the organization. She then created teams that have quietly been remaking the campus. All the while, she has been infusing individuals with a sense of organizational identity, camaraderie, and purpose in an institution that had sorely missed it.

The portrait of the first leader is of the white knight who came to clean up and solve problems. The problems were seen as people, the staff and faculty. The second leader is someone who sets the stage for good actions to occur by fomenting dialogue, trusting individuals, and creating structures that will enable people to work with one another. Both presidents focused on goals and performance, but one sought immediate change without a view to the future and the other focused on the present and the future.

Teams

One way to create structures in which people will work together is through teams. The work of a team of and by itself will not solve a particular problem or reform the organization. Too often, we rigidly rely on the latest management fad as a quick fix to long-term problems that plague the organization. If a leader thinks of himself as the old-fashioned coach and everyone else as a member of the team, then he will not be successful at redesign by the invocation of a desire for "teamwork." A team that works in isolation to solve a problem that demands a systemic solution is merely a variation of old-time decision making; it fails to live up to the potential that teams offer the organization. One way of thinking about teams is as a component of the strategic design, rather than the magic cure-all. In this light, soft projects work in consort with the overall organizational plans and line decision-makers, rather than in isolation.

I also should point out what teams are not. In particular, there are five vantage points from which we should not approach teams.

1. *Teams and teamwork are not the same.* Recognize that such words do not have meaning until they are put into practice. The suggestion that a leader wants *teamwork* may imply little more than the leader wants people to pull together and get along. A nice suggestion; however, it does not speak to a fundamentally different way of redesigning organizational action.

2. *Teams without results attached to them become conversations.* Simply creating a team does not change an organization. Teams come together for a reason. Think of the examples offered with regard to soft projects—low enrollments and curricular change. Specific goals need to be created for which the team will work; the team is the process used to achieve the goals. Without such goals individuals in a team tend to waste their time. Teams in redesigned organizations focus on performance.

3. *Teams are not "group think."* One danger of teams can be that those individuals in the minority or who have different ideas are cast aside in the rush to solve problems and work together. Such actions are mistakes. One of President Kennedy's main errors in the Bay of Pigs, for example, was surrounding himself with individuals who all held similar views of the world as he did. Teams need to be process-oriented and working toward goals, but they also need to be designed so that they stimulate creative thinking from individuals who diverge from the norm.

4. *Teams are not Noah's Ark.* A team is certainly not a dyad, but more often than not I see the opposite; we choose one from here, one from there, and end up with a mishmash of interest and potential. Rules are made to be broken, but my rule of thumb is to try to stick to no more than 10 individuals, and preferably seven when we create a team. The size of the organization is certainly a factor, but if a team is to work together, they are going to meet on a regular basis and they need to know one another. When I know others depend upon me, I am less likely to find a reason to miss a meeting. When I am in a group the size of a council meeting at the United Nations, I know that my voice will not be missed if I have other pressing tasks.

5. *Teams are not all the same.* Teams, like cultures, are unique. They take on the characteristics and personalities of the individuals who account for the team. In particular, they often become structured according to the facilitator's proclivities. I raise this point because leaders ought not to expect a manual for teams as if they are giving someone lessons on how to drive a car. No two teams will be alike. I tend to be punctual, so when I facilitate a team our working arrangement begins and ends at stated times. Other teams will function in a different manner. The focus ought not be on the inner workings of the individuals who account for the team, but on the goals they have set for themselves and whether they have achieved them. Focus on outcomes and process.

I earlier noted the importance of process in the role of a leader. Teams also must constantly be focused on goals. Faculty meetings are all too often consumed by conversations and dialogue that never move toward closure. Teams in postsecondary organizations especially need to develop a style for team work so that when people come together something has been improved upon by the meeting's end. Teams constantly ask themselves, "What has been accomplished?" Frequently, the only such answer in a college committee meeting will be that they have set the date for their next meeting. This is not good enough. Teams should be results-oriented.

Teams are structures that bring people together across diverse areas. They begin with three principles:

1. They have a sense of a problem.

2. They recognize that they need to solve the problem.

3. They acknowledge that they need measures to assess how the solution is working at specific points in time.

Teams operate through facilitative interaction; process is geared toward outcomes. As stated earlier, leaders do not create teams merely to make people feel as if they are a part of the process. On occasion some parents will sit their children down and discuss where they should take their vacation. True, children have some input in this process, but the parents drive the car or buy tickets for the plane. No one fools himself about who is in charge. Organizations should not be thought of as families where mothers and fathers, college and university presidents, make the decisions for the children, the faculty, and the staff. A commitment to teams necessitates a flatter organization. Teams are accorded power and authority with the assumption that those closest to the decision have the best capability of making the right decision if they accept the responsibility accorded to them. The leader's challenge is to imbue the organization and the teams with that sense of responsibility and to facilitate their ability to come up with good results.

I have pointed out here the dual and contradictory role of a leader. On the one hand the leader sets design; on the other hand he or she creates the conditions for teams to evolve. Some leaders might create teams, but still feel compelled to state the team's purpose, define the goals, and outline the process that will be used to achieve the goals. Here the leader has set sail correctly, but cannot break the habit of being the ship's captain who sets the direction. Others may call teams together because they want people to provide input, but offer no guidance or input. Without communicating high expectations or rules of behavior in this scenario, the leader is setting the group up for failure.

I also have pointed out how the leader needs to concentrate on process in order to achieve high performance. A focus on design without a sense of organizational purpose becomes little more than an architectural performance. A concern for goals at the expense of process achieves short-term gains at the cost of long-term redesign.

I suggested that certain pitfalls or dangers exist with teams. Individuals may feel that they lose their autonomy. Innovation could actually decrease or be stifled if teams become enmeshed in everyone's agreeing with one another. Politics is always a problem; individuals trade favors with one another and lose sight of high performance outcomes as they race to best one another within or across teams. No structure is foolproof. The work of organizations is the work of life. Teams offer a way to redesign radically how people conduct the work of the organization. Although teams are not the answer, without them I am unconvinced an organization will be able to redesign. The linchpin is the leader who is able to calibrate his or her power and authority and create the conditions for teams to occur, to develop goals, to create the route to those goals, and to develop a way to assess performance.

Leadership Quiz 2

1. What is the image I have for myself as a leader?
2. How comfortable am I allowing those individuals whom I think of as below me in the organizational structure to make decisions?
3. What is the single greatest barrier for the success of teams here and what can I do to remove the barrier?

Executing Change

Let me begin, rather than end, this section with the following quiz questions.

Leadership Quiz 3

1. What is the mission of my institution?
2. What are its core values?
3. Give one example where an outsider would see the mission or a core value at work.

A college president who works at a conservative Christian institution that I have studied might be able to come up with a clear response to the questions in the Leadership Quiz 3. "Our mission is to serve students and their families by promoting the teachings of Jesus Christ. We believe in the sanctity of human life and creationism. Everyone attends a daily worship service, classes frequently begin with a prayer, and the curriculum reflects our beliefs that practices such as abortion and homosexuality are morally wrong."

I am not suggesting that all colleges necessarily adopt any of those specific points if they are to successfully answer the quiz. However, consider the individual at the public state college that I have also studied who says, "We are for educational excellence and we want to be ranked as the best. We value diversity. A walk through our campus will point out the new addition to the library; all faculty offices are wired for the Internet, and we have a lab in the new wing for students which shows our commitment to the future."

Think of a business whose the chief executive officer is able to say, "Our mission is to offer our customers the most user-friendly software on the market at affordable prices. We value our customers and we have worked to ensure that no one has to wait more than 60 seconds when they place a phone call to us. If they are not satisfied with the product they buy, or the service they receive, we will refund their money."

A mission needs to be specific enough so that in a state of crisis, those who work for the organization believe in what they are doing to the extent that they will not drop the mission at the first sign of trouble. A core value is similar. If a value is not central, then it is possible to change it without any concern. I am not saying that institutions with clear missions and values are static. Clearly, they change. However, in organizations that have deeply held beliefs a crisis does not mean that its values change. If they do, the organization is undergoing a dramatic ideological shift that one may experience only once every generation, if at all.

The conservative Christian university will not be a Christian institution if it changes its mission. The same is true with respect to its values. A business that has built consumer confidence by offering affordable merchandise in a customer-friendly atmosphere will dig itself in a deeper hole if it abandons such values. We have no way of knowing, however, what educational excellence or a commitment to diversity means at a public institution. A vision and value that is as broad as *excellence* or *diversity* can easily be adapted to changing marketplaces. Perhaps, then, the public institution is the one that is best suited for redesign because it will be the easiest to change? Soft projects seem to suggest that ideas come and go. Perhaps leadership by design implies creating a broad enough framework so that colleges and universities are able to expand and contract without going through the organizational angst that the Christian institution or the customer-friendly company will experience?

The Importance of Mission Statements

The best examples of clear mission statements are those of institutions that Burton Clark (1980) has defined as "distinctive." As the overriding ethos of the organization's culture, a mission statement helps people make sense of who they are as an institution and where they want to go. A mission statement not only raises questions about which direction the institution should move in the future, but it also offers answers.

We need to expand our notions of what a mission is so that the organization's participants do not equate a mission simply with formulaic goals and objectives. The mission should incorporate the aspirations and hopes of the community and define who they serve. Mission statements link up an organization's history with present-day contexts to provide a vision of the future. In this sense, mission statements are future-oriented. The mission of an organization also helps provide guidelines for action within its culture, while at the same time calling into question how activities might change in the future. In effect, a mission is a rallying point that needs to highlight how a group of individuals, faculty, staff, and administrators, have come together in order to help a specific group, such as students and parents, achieve a particular goal.

The example of the Christian institution helps participants understand how the organization is unique; they gain a sense of the parameters of the culture. The same is true with the company that offers customer-friendly affordable software. We cannot make that claim at an institution that has a mission which would fit virtually any institution anywhere. The leader continually needs to ask, What is unique about this institution? The mission serves as a reference point for change so that the participants question how their work relates to the work of the institution. To avoid talking about the mission or to overlook it as irrelevant and a waste of time denies participants a sense of organizational meaning. In this light, what I am calling for is an extension of Clark's (1980) notion of saga. He notes that

> . . .an embodied idea is the institutional chariot to which individual motive becomes chained. . . . In such efforts, the task—and the reward—of the institutional leader is to create and initiate an activating mission. (p. 262)

What, then, does a leader do to create a mission statement? An organization's participants need to think of a mission statement as an internally generated document that expresses to the world who they are. A statement such as "We wish to be the best public university in the country," is more an externally generated comment than one that is internal. Reputational mission statements about excellence, being number one, or being a leader hinge on what others will say about the organization rather than what the organization says about themselves. "The vision statement expresses the contribution we want to make to the organization," notes Peter Block, "not what the external world is going to bestow on us" (Block, 1987, p. 115). The focus is on who we are to ourselves. It has more to do with making sense to the organization's participants than as a marketing ploy to attract notice. Once the organization's participants know who they are and who they serve, they will be able to communicate that knowledge by action.

In a college or university the mission statement should also focus on two complementary issues: people and ideas (Tierney, 1998). The leader needs to activate discussion about who the audience is and how to serve them. Similarly, the organization's participants need some sense of what kind of idea ties the organization together. The Christian university has a clear answer to both queries; it serves Christian students and offers a curriculum linked to a conservative religious worldview. The computer company has a similarly clear response; it serves customers who seek inexpensive, well-designed software. Undoubtedly, there are countless examples that an institution might develop. One college might say they serve the urban area and have a curriculum linked to explicit forms of employment. Another institution might say they want students who desire work in the public sector, so they offer an education with explicit linkages to a liberal form of social democracy.

A mission statement also enables a group to confirm how its members will work with and treat one another. For example, one cannot lay claim to "educating students to work in a democracy" if one's organization is not democratically run. An organization that subscribes to religious principles needs to live by them or the mission becomes a sham. A public university that seeks to promote multiculturalism will appear foolish, if not hypocritical, if the organization is not populated with people of color. In effect, the leader's task is to ensure that what they say is what we do.

Finally, an organization's participants need a mission statement that points people in two ostensibly different directions. One direction is grand and sweeping; the statement inspires people and rallies them around a grand cause. A mission statement is not the place to itemize or create objectives. Nevertheless, what flows from a worthy mission statement is a sense of where organizational units and individuals will focus. As Peter Drucker (1990) has observed, "A mission statement has to be operational, otherwise it's just good intentions" (p. 4). In effect, a mission statement should enable teams to come together to create a finite list of core values that exemplify how they will focus their energies.

Core Values

I stated earlier that one role for a design leader is to help teams focus their efforts. No focus could be more helpful than to ensure that the values the organization and units develop are finite and firm. One pitfall of colleges and universities is creating multiple values that bump into one another en route to being enacted, or more likely, are discarded because an organization's participants cannot adhere to an infinite number of principles.

Core values flow from the mission and are finite, broadly shared, and clearly understood. In times of stress they are not simply dropped. A core value of a private liberal arts college might be that all classes are taught by tenure line professors in classes of no more than 40 because this college defines good teaching as the ability to create a personal relationship between teacher and student. The faculty and administration must believe that the value is true, that it is a central aspect of who they are, and they need to be able to put the value into action. The implications of such a value have obvious ramifications for the entire college. If teaching assistants and part-time faculty teach a majority of entry level under-graduate courses, senior faculty teach only graduate courses, or large classes become the norm, then clearly how the academic citizens define good teaching has changed.

Similarly, when an institution notes that it will have an active relationship with the business community so that its students have jobs, it is creating an equally defining statement. A value that says "we are consumer-oriented" means that students cannot find faculty absent from their offices or secretaries who do not answer the phones. There may well be good reasons why faculty or secretaries are absent, but if those reasons take precedence over consumer service, then the organization ought not have service as a core value. "Core" means *core*, not *nice if we have the time and money*.

The path to developing core values is for the leader to design a mechanism where teams are able to discuss openly and freely how they intend to enact the mission by the values they espouse. Once individuals have developed such values, then the leader needs to reiterate them in multiple venues and manners. A one-time speech at the start of the school year will not impress upon people what the institution holds important. Simply speaking to alumnae will not convey to everyone the values that the organization holds. In effect, what needs to occur is for the leader to design ways where abstractions such as mission statements and values are put into play by way of clear, consistent examples throughout the organization.

I asked earlier if mission statements and explicitly held values might be anathema to reengineering and soft projects. What I have highlighted in this chapter, however, is the need in times of significant structural change for a sense in the organization of who *we* are, what the organization's participants believe, and what they hope to accomplish. The word *hope* is not loosely applied; organizational cultures are configurations of individual and collective dreams. I have pointed out that this is the case even more today since academics currently invest more time and energy in their colleges and universities than before.

Missions and values ought not to be conceived of as organizational straitjackets any more than a religion or nation's beliefs are. Certainly, one is able to find cults where individuals are indoctrinated, but not all religions and not all nations have such ethos. The same is true with an organization. Undoubtedly, someone will find an organization that holds on to its mission and values so tightly that it is unable to keep pace with the times and will close. The art of administration is always one of balance.

The emphasis on an organization's mission and values, however, forces individuals to think about the balance. The payoffs are two-fold. On the one hand individuals become self-referential about what is important to them and what they are able to concentrate and focus on. On the other hand, they are able to provide meaning throughout turbulent times. Individuals need something to hold onto when they are asked to change the way they do business. Organizational redesign calls for a dramatically different framework. Individuals are aided when they sense that the design is intended to help the organization improve on what they consider key, essential, and valuable. The leader, then, communicates where the group is going, and at the same time creates the climate for individuals to come together as teams and develop strategies and goals that put into action the group's collective hopes and values.

The Parameters of Planning

Belasco and Stayer (1993) note, "Vision alone is no solution. Everything is execution" (p. 31). I could not agree more. I have often met dreamers who are able to sketch beautiful structures that ultimately are built on little more than shifting sands. Words have meanings; they also must suggest actions. True, a vision statement or a mission that delineates core values of the institution is meant in part to stimulate people, to bring them together, and to work toward a common goal. At the same time, if we do not see actions that derive from these values, then the words ring hollow.

I have visited campuses where the president has initiated a strategic planning process that consumes a better part of an academic year talking about vision and mission. By the time the conversation finishes, the entire campus has become sick of the process and decides that it needs to get on with the "real work." In effect, the work of the mission became decoupled from the day-to-day affairs of the institution; ultimately, because countless hours were spent on the process, it ended up as a waste of time. How, then, to proceed?

Unlike mission statements, which I encouraged us to think of with regard to *hope,* planning is what we *do.* Goals are the endpoints; they are operational rather than visionary. and they are made operational by objectives. One role of leadership mentioned earlier is to lay out a framework for action and to encourage teams to function in effective ways. It is wishful thinking to simply throw a group of people together and assume they will produce effective policies and plans that relate to the mission and then carry through on those plans. Leaders need to constantly nurture teams and work with them to ensure productivity. Although there are no rules for how to develop a planning process and implement goals in a postsecondary organization, there are seven points to consider when an organization's participants move from vision statements to planning and goals.

1. Time Frame

People need to know the temporal parameters of the process and what they need to accomplish within a set time frame. Committee work seems to consume hours of individual time and nothing is ever accomplished except that individuals meet at appointed times. Rather than begin a discussion as if time is of no consequence, in an organization where reengineering is important, tasks need to be developed with endpoints in mind.

A time frame also underscores that these issues are critical, important, and perhaps urgent. As Katzenbach and Smith (1994) point out, "The more urgent and meaningful the rationale, the more likely it is that a real team will emerge" (p. 119). The leader's role is to establish a sense of urgency, and reiterate that the work of the committee matters and will be honored. Nothing can be more self-defeating than pulling a group of busy people together and consuming their time with ill-defined issues that serve no useful purpose and achieve no specific goal other than to say that they have met.

2. Decision Making

Colleges and universities differ from businesses and corporations in their decision-making structures. Indeed, one of the centerpieces of academic life is the role faculty have in the governance of the institution. However, as anyone knows who has participated in collegial decision making, shared governance can be confusing and maddening. It need not be so. The first step toward improving faculty governance is to clarify who makes decisions and where final decisions lie.

Colleges and universities do not need a long-winded, formalized document that individuals turn to for guidance on every issue that arises before them. However, when an organization begins to redesign, the participants need to be clear about who is involved in the decision and who is not. Similarly, there is also the need to be cognizant of the time frame involved. What troubles me is that issues often arise in a faculty forum and no one is exactly clear why one particular committee is agreeing to it and another is not; once the committee has voted on it, people are then unclear where to send the policy for final approval.

Often, how faculty make decisions takes on greater importance than the actual decision itself. Faculty also tend to talk decisions to death unless consensus is reached. Faculty might agree to hold to the principle that the collegium is a representative democracy where voting takes place. It is unhelpful to the change process to assume that unless everyone agrees the organization cannot proceed. Rather, individuals need to begin the discussion of issues with a sense of how issues will be resolved and within what time frame.

3. From Critique to Proposal

Faculty are versed in the art of critique. They find what is weak in an argument and outline in detail what is wrong. I mentioned earlier that when leaders develop teams they surely want a full-bodied discussion that entails the back and forth that is so common in faculty dialogues. At the same time, faculty need to move from merely criticizing what is wrong with an idea to a dialogue that outlines what possibly might be right.

More troubling than a faculty who merely criticizes issues is the increasing likelihood that proposals derive solely from administrative ideas. Faculty work becomes reduced to the reaction to ideas instead of the development of their own ideas. One of the strengths of team-oriented work that has definable time frames and goals is the active structured solicitation of faculty input on a wide variety of issues.

Obviously, simply saying that faculty should offer more constructive ideas is not going to make it happen. One of the roles of the leader is to ensure that faculty feel part of the process and to gently nudge the proceedings along. Communication becomes essential, rather than unnecessary. Faculty often feel as if the administration has provided too short a time frame for an idea to be fully discussed. The administration, having worked on the idea for a great while, feels frustrated that their good idea is not quickly acted on and implemented. This all-too-frequent scenario need not occur if the strategy that leaders enact is full participation of faculty within the confines of teamwork and time frames.

4. Focus

As I will elaborate in Chapter 3, an organization's participants can handle only a finite number of topics. It serves no one well if an organization jumps from topic to topic reacting to different emergencies. A leader's task is to keep teams focused on the issues that brought them together. All too often discussion moves from issue *a* to *b* to *z* with blinding rapidity, and individuals end up spending time and energy on issues that have little to do with a task at hand. Similarly, decision-makers often will spend as much time discussing how a form should be rewritten as what they want to do with regard to restructuring academic departments. What needs to occur is an initial clarifying statement about what is expected and continuous feedback about how progress is occurring on the initial topic as individuals move toward closure at an expected deadline.

5. Outcomes

Plans have consequences. Faculty and administrators must be concerned with the outcomes of their work, rather than merely the efforts they have expended. This principle is clear in the tenure system where a candidate undergoes a rigorous review. However hard the individual may have worked, he or she most likely will not receive tenure if teaching, research, and service are mediocre. And whenever possible, the organization's participants ought to set specific collective expectations. If a mission statement should stop saying "we're number one," or "we will increase production by 200%," then plans need to delineate what is meant by excellence or quality and the like. Numbers should not come out of thin air.

A college experiences an enrollment decline and has 3,300 students. The team involved in enrollment decides that next year they need to increase enrollment to 4,000. Why? No other reason exists except that the number is the next largest thousand. Setting goals in this manner is whimsical, arbitrary, and ultimately harmful. Perhaps the college would be able to recruit more individuals; if so, then they are shortchanging themselves. Perhaps the number is so far out of reason that they will fall short by half, yet that increase will be sufficient to enable a healthy organization. The result is that people feel badly that they did not meet their goal, even though their only mistake was in picking an arbitrary number rather than a more reasoned one.

I am not necessarily suggesting that individuals set goals with exact precision, because such an act may be so time-consuming that they end up with the right number but no time to reach it. One of the leader's roles is to expect specific numeric outcomes and outline a plan to achieve them that seems logical. Goals that have numbers attached to them also enable individuals to monitor periodic progress. The point is not merely to pick a lottery ticket in September and hope that it hits in June, but to attach a process to a goal and enable everyone to see how they are doing along the way.

6. The Ethnographic Eye

I am advocating an intense form of working relationships that can develop organizational excitement and camaraderie and ultimately produce demonstrable goals. Organizations run two risks that pertain to what I will call internal and external myopia. On the one hand, a team may become so engaged in their task that they forget to advertise their ideas and progress with the rest of the academic community. Such a flaw can be fatal in an organization that thrives on rumor and lives (and dies) by shared governance. "What are those people doing over there?" will be heard. "I heard they're thinking of eliminating _____." Fill in the blank.

External myopia pertains to individuals who come together to develop a plan about a particular topic, and then go about their business without any realization that other individuals on other campuses have worked on quite similar topics. Leaders should not want their institutions merely to mimic what someone else has done, but neither should they want either to reinvent the wheel or ignore information that might be helpful to particular tasks.

Leaders need to enable information to flow freely to multiple constituencies throughout the process and also to enable individuals to develop a comparative perspective. I admire an organization's participants when they develop a unique approach to a problem, especially if they are aware that they have developed something unique. I am suggesting that leaders try to avoid having other participants in the organizations unaware of what is taking place. Also, leaders need to help individuals avoid making decisions that would have appeared foolhardy if the individuals had only thought to look beyond their organization's borders.

The leader with an ethnographic eye constantly reflects on organizational processes and goals. Such leaders think internally about how the culture of the organization is being nurtured and what needs to change. They also develop reflection by looking beyond their campuses into other venues.

Leadership Quiz 4

1. What are three central projects that were discussed and implemented in the last 12 months at your institution?
2. What was the role of the faculty in the decision to implement these projects?
3. How are you evaluating the success of these projects?

Ownership

I end in many respects where I began this chapter, with the idea of ownership. Organizations do not reside in the shadows of great men or women. Colleges and universities also are not simply aimless entities that wander from issue to issue; if they are, they will not survive the present and future challenges I outlined in the Introduction. Academic institutions vitally need leaders who are able to disengage their egos, pride, and prerogatives from the office itself and instead think of themselves as designers who create ownership on the part of the organization's constituents. Peter Block (1987) cogently observes, "We commit to that which we own. . . . We create ownership/commitment when we give others freedom to choose their own path to achieving results, [and] structure work so that people are doing a whole job instead of a piece of a job" (p. 83).

The task of this chapter has been discussing how to enable leaders to develop and maintain a vision and organizational identity, and then to put grand ideas into practice by way of strategic teamwork. In the next chapter I expand on the idea of focus by discussing an organizational malady that has become all too common in academe, and consider a curative.

3

Organizational Attention Deficit Disorder

Evaluating High Performance

Now, here, you see, it takes all the running you can do, to keep in the same place. If you want to get somewhere else, you must run at least twice as fast as that!

—Lewis Carroll, *Through the Looking Glass*

My brother, a successful investment banker, called me once and spoke about a business he had just acquired. "It's a small company," he said. "The investment was easy and we've made a killing. Paper money, though. But the profits are certain. It's a great deal. So how are you doing? How's the university doing?" I spoke about papers published and articles to be written, and about the toils and tribulations of working in a private university at the close of the 20th century. "But what's the bottom line," he interrupted impatiently. "Is the university doing well or not?"

A friend works with a fellow in another part of the country who has not published anything in more than 5 years. "The guy seems to be working," my friend bemoaned, "but there are no results. He's off in the library or rewriting this or that at home. But it's never finished. It's maddening."

At another institution, a colleague works in a school of humanities that has experienced a 15% enrollment decline over 12 months. A state of emergency has set in, and the provost recently asked to see the dean. The dean and a small "crisis-management team" have devised a plan that will close a new department and merge six departments into three divisions. Senior faculty joke that when they first arrived they had divisions and a decade ago had created departments, so now they are back to square one.

The provost reviewed the plan and wondered if the quality of the school would rise. As she noted, "I'm worried about academic quality and I don't see anything in here that addresses those concerns." The dean and his team have gone back to the drawing board.

These scenarios frame the content of this chapter. Participants in academe have long puzzled over how to evaluate higher education's "bottom line," as my brother so desires. Once upon a time, faculty and administrators ridiculed calls for such analyses, and when asked replied, "We are not a business. We don't have bottom lines." Well enough. Colleges and universities were not a business 100 years ago, and they are not a business today. Nevertheless, the negative response "We are not a business" is no longer sufficient. We need some sense of how we are doing and how we might improve in order to maintain excellence.

The professor who works hard but never produces is also an organizational conundrum. The easiest response has been to let such people alone. "I mind my own business," the feeling goes, "and you mind yours." Such a credo is especially appealing to academics who often think of their work as individualistic. They entered academe in part to be left alone. However, such intellectual isolation in the academic workplace is harmful to the individual and to the community. Academics ought not to ignore the relationships and obligations they have to one another as members of an academic community. Also, an organization's participants cannot overlook issues of productivity and effectiveness at a time when every individual's effort is essential.

And finally, the provost's demand for a plan that solves enrollment problems and ends up focusing on quality may appear to be a logical thread to the provost, but not to anyone else. The dean and his school have become involved in what organizational theorists define as a "garbage can model of decision-making," where they begin with one problem that evolves into work on completely different matters.

How does an organization's participants know how they are doing? What are indicators of organizational excellence if they cannot use bottom lines? Is the effort involved in writing an article sufficient for a professor, or ought the expectation be something more from a faculty member, such as a published piece? How does the organization maintain its focus? In

Chapters 1 and 2, I outlined what I meant by high performance and organizational redesign. But as John Garvin has asked, "How will managers know when their companies have become learning organizations?" (1991, p. 79). The intent of this chapter is to come to terms with this question. I first focus on the problem and why we have been unable to answer it. I then define *effectiveness* in high performance organizations, and conclude by outlining five steps necessary for evaluation.

Attention Deficit Disorder

For over a decade, researchers have pointed out how some individuals suffer from what is called *attention deficit disorder*. A child's inability to concentrate, inattention to detail, and desire to skip from topic to topic frequently make learning difficult, if not impossible. Hyperactivity often masks problems of not knowing how to concentrate and accomplish what one has set out to do.

Sound familiar? Many individuals talk about colleges and universities in the same manner. Postsecondary organizations tend to be unable to concentrate on one topic over a long time period; an organization's participants do not focus on details or outcomes; they often seem at one and the same time to be hyperactive and running in place. What they learn about themselves as members of an organization is equally difficult, if not impossible. If a child has an inability to learn when he or she has such problems, then surely participants in an organization will be unable to become a learning organization when they demonstrate similar characteristics.

I by no means wish to trivialize a disorder that many children apparently have and that can be quite serious when untreated. If anything, the discovery of such a problem in individuals enables us to think of how such a problem also confronts collectivities. A postsecondary institution's inability to orchestrate coherent, consistent action and its desire to drop one strategic plan and pick up another one at a whim are both signs of an organization that can neither be reengineered nor effectively evaluated. What accounts for organizational attention deficit disorder? (See Table 3.1.) What are the symptoms and how might it be cured? Doctors frequently prescribe Ritalin® for children; what might be suggested for a college or university?

TABLE 3.1 Symptoms of An Organization Out of Focus (Goleman, 1990)

Restlessness:	Inability to stay focused on a goal.
Distractibility:	Inability to keep the organizational culture focused on the task; forgetfulness.
Mood swings:	Shifting from depression to mild elation.
Disorganization:	Inability to finish tasks; switching from task to task haphazardly; disorganization in solving problems or managing time.
Impulsivity:	Making decisions with little reflection or too little information; abruptly beginning and ending tasks; foolish investments; recklessness.
Low tolerance for stress:	Daily life seems a constant crisis.

Preventive Medicine and Evaluation

An organization's participants usually continue to think of evaluation as an activity that comes after an action has occurred. "How was the movie?" someone might ask, and then evaluate it. At the end of the course, instructors provide students with an evaluation. After a candidate toils for 6 years, his or her peers evaluate the individual's dossier and decide whether to grant tenure to the person. Those who write grant applications inevitably include an evaluation component stating that when the project is over, they will tell the grantor whether the project actually did what it purported to do.

Formative rather than summative evaluation has gained credence over the last generation. Instructors might provide a midcourse evaluation in their classes in order to correct deficiencies for the remaining half of the course. Tenure candidates often have a 3-year review, though admittedly more often than not, such reviews are perfunctory. Similarly, grant proposals speak about "ongoing evaluation" activities, but often, the funding is so tight that getting the project up and running is enough of a struggle. Researchers have neither the resources nor the energy to develop a formative assessment. Indeed, most often evaluation devolves to little more than functional reporting: "We said we would hold x activities and we held them; we agreed to interview y families and we did."

The same problems plague organizational assessment. Individuals often have enough problems implementing change. Who has time to stop and assess how they are doing, or whether they are doing what they said they would be doing? An organization's participants need every possible hand to help build the project and set it afloat. To have someone step back and evaluate the construction from any number of angles seems to be a luxury that is simply not affordable.

A college decides to overhaul its general educational program, for example, and a 2-year discussion ensues, complete with political intrigue, intellectual obfuscation, and mountains of data that analyze college course patterns from any number of angles. At the end of 2 years, the college has a new general education curriculum, and everyone claims success. The goal was to put a new curriculum in place, and it was accomplished. But no one has developed a way to monitor whether the curricular changes achieve what they set out to do. Instead, the curriculum moves along and evolves without any sense of formalized assessment. The norm becomes that once individuals have one problem solved, another crops up and they are off and running.

By and large, academic organizations have not learned what has become clear about an individual's physical health. A person ought not to wait until he or she is too ill to seek a cure. An institution's participants also do not need to place the maintenance of the organization's health in the hands of external experts, although, at times, akin to a visit to the doctor, such advice is necessary. Nevertheless, faculty and administrators need to learn how to assess their organizational health in an ongoing informal manner, and at periodic times during the course of an academic year. "Anyone," note Adams and Peck (1996), "can examine what they do day-to-day, improve on it, and enroll others to do things more effectively" (p. 15). I am suggesting that an organization's participants think of evaluation as a crucial activity; as something that comes first. Evaluation begins the moment actions occur, and those who are in the organization need to learn to monitor their organization's health.

Motivation

An individual who suffers from attention deficit disorder focuses on compensatory behavioral strategies such as keeping daily lists of what he or she needs to accomplish and holding on to a daily appointment calendar. An organization should focus its energies and motivate its personnel in a similar fashion. Colleges and universities need to create goals that are broadly shared and understood, define tasks so that individuals comprehend what is expected of them and what they believe they can accomplish, and then reward behavior for accomplishment of the task rather than merely for the effort.

People cannot perform well if the goals of the organization and the tasks they are asked to perform change at the drop of a hat. If in the fall semester, for example, faculty are told that their top priority should be recruiting students, and then in the spring they are told that actually their number one priority should be proposal development, then neither goal will be reached. The culture of the organization needs to sustain, nurture, and enhance an understanding of what the organization is about and what they hope to accomplish.

Insularity in a global economy is also a sure path to failure. Periodic, strategic reviews of the environment enable individuals to gain information that extends beyond their boundaries so that the kind of redesign discussed in Chapter 1 is possible. As importantly, individuals also become aware of how other entities perform and have some kind of reference for their own actions.

Although people need information about the culture of the organization and the events that circumscribe organizational action, they also need to know that they have the ability to make decisions for those activities and events that are within their purview. Individuals need to develop the capacity to think of issues not as segmented and cordoned off from one another. They also must recognize that more often than not, the individuals closest to the action have the best idea about how to solve the problem. If they do not, then the organization's leaders have not provided them with the information or skills necessary to accomplish their work. If individuals are unable to do so, then they should not be assigned the task. If the organizational ethos does not allow them to make the decisions, then the ethos must change.

Similarly, although organizational cultures need to nurture creativity and the ability for individuals to garner information and make decisions, organizations also need cultures that reward people for their work. Such a statement is deceptively simple. On the one hand, as I will elaborate in the next chapter, across-the-board pay increases should be an artifact of the past. For Professor Jones merely to survive another year ought not to justify a raise, especially if one's colleague has worked and performed exceedingly hard while Professor Jones has not.

On the other hand, rewards also have to be connected with a climate in which the organization's participants not only focus on achievement but also reward risk-taking. If they reward only those individuals who "produce," then the organization will create a culture of minimalists. An intellectual organization, a learning community, must comprise a collection of risk-takers who study, teach, and work in ways that are experimental, innovative, and unique. Of necessity, some experiments fail. However, the innovator may well deserve a raise if the organization seeks to reward those who develop an idea and run with it. If a college or university provides pay increases only for those who stick by the status quo, then the organization will never find individuals who seek to cross boundaries, work on soft projects, or attempt new designs.

Rewards are also not tied solely to monetary gain. A climate that nurtures its personnel is one that maintains a constant focus on the psychological well-being of the organization. Again, one way out of attention deficit disorder is by the maintenance of a self-referential system that applauds actions when goals are reached and creates a sense of individual well-being, autonomy, and worth.

Stasis and Mountain Climbing

I have a friend who is overweight, but seemingly healthy. When I once suggested that he go to the gym, he commented, "My grandmother smoked a pack of cigarettes a day and drank vodka, and her favorite food was bacon and fried eggs. She lived until she was 93." I gather the moral of his story was that he planned to live as she did, and exercise was irrelevant because he had good genes.

Another friend who is in his early forties is not overweight, but does absolutely no exercise. A brisk 15-minute walk in the park to him is a monumental effort. He commented to me once, "I wouldn't know how to begin. And besides, I don't have the time, energy, or stamina. I'm fine the way I am."

I am not an exercise guru. I also do not want to stretch the analogy of individual and organizational health. However, as with my friend, I do not believe organizations are "fine the way we are." Similarly, my overweight friend assumes that perhaps other individuals need to stay in shape, but he is different. True, some organizations do have a history of robust health. However, for the reasons provided in the introduction, stasis is no longer sufficient. High performance demands an environment that continually seeks to improve on what the organization is doing. A high performance organization has participants who are never content to survive; they must thrive. I am positing an organizational climate wherein faculty and administrators are mountain climbers in search of new vistas and new challenges, rather than merely pedestrians who assume that what they are doing is good enough.

What does it suggest for an organization that seeks to evaluate itself to use the principles of preventive medicine, motivation, and action, rather than reaction? How do such principles enable individuals to decide how they are doing or how an individual is performing, or how to decide what to do? Such principles are a framework for action, a *way* of thinking about how to evaluate. I now turn to how to ground such a framework in evaluative mechanisms.

Employing Effectiveness: Eyes on the Prize

Perhaps nowhere is the disjuncture between theory and research greater than with effectiveness and high performance. Several excellent scholarly works exist that help define what the meaning of effectiveness or quality from multiple perspectives (e.g., Cameron, 1978; Cameron & Whetten, 1996; Haworth & Conrad, 1997). The problem is that in the "real world" of academic environments, as I mentioned above, administrators, staff, and faculty seldom have time to deal with the intricacies of one or another approach that utilizes microscopic analytic techniques. The concerns in academe certainly do not defy analysis or measurement. Nevertheless, academic work demands techniques and procedures specific to college and university life, and not theoretical formulas or abstract statistical measurements that might do well for graduate seminars on the one hand, or profit-making companies on the other.

In my work I am often asked to find out "how we are doing." What might be studied to answer such a question? What indicators will give an organization's participants assurance that a unit is a high performer? I offer five tools to use.

Management by Fact

Although I may not need statistical data in a manner akin to a for-profit company that defines excellence, I am also uncomfortable when people say, "We are good," and basically suggest that I trust their judgment. I point out to individuals that if their son or daughter asked for advice about a particular professor, department, or activity on their campus, they would try to steer them in a particular way. They would say, "Don't take Smith, take Jones," and would offer that judgment based on what they know about Smith and Jones. Smith may not prepare for his classes and may be a boring teacher, while Jones might be innovative, friendly, and rigorous.

The same points can be made about virtually any activity or group on campus. Men and women make evaluative judgments all the time. Rather than calling on blind faith, individuals are merely making explicit what many people implicitly believe is true. Sometimes, someone's implicit assumptions are off base, so evaluative dialogues help correct errors. At other times, what individuals kept to themselves is not commonly known and accepted, so what they are doing is letting others in on knowledge that they have previously held secret.

Any academic administrator also knows the nightmare of comparability. A call goes out from the provost's office that a small pot of money will be awarded to a school or college that demonstrates excellence. One school bases its definition of quality on publications and distinguished faculty, another on grants brought in, a third on service to the community, and a fourth on its national ranking in a magazine. Clearly, they are dealing with apples and oranges here. Without any common criteria for excellence, departments are free to make their cases in any way they see as advantageous.

Any department chair or dean has had similarly mind-boggling exercises with individual faculty as they have struggled to determine who deserves a raise, a summer stipend, or a particular award. One professor comments that he has more students in his classes than anyone; a second relates how she has more dissertation advisees than the rest of her department; and a colleague points out that he brought in a significant grant that helped the college in innumerable ways. Which is the correct decision? What data do we call on?

Two points rise to the surface when one wades into such turbulent waters. First, everyone needs broad organizational direction and guidance. Second, the diversity that exists in academe is both a reality that needs to be reckoned with and something to be welcomed.

Academic community involves more than simply everyone "doing his or her own thing." Colleges and universities are no longer in an environment where an individual's good idea will be automatically funded or supported. This suggests that individuals need guidance about what they are expected to do. Mission statements and strategic principles offer one clue about what they should do. Leaders who communicate and reiterate themes in their daily work provide another clue. That is, a president, dean, or chair who emphasizes that service to the surrounding community is valued offers guidance about where he or she wants the institution to focus. Laundry lists do not work; individuals and groups generally can hold three to five key ideas.

At the same time, there is nothing necessarily wrong if a philosophy department defines its excellence by its intellectual reputation, a chemistry department by its external funding, and an education department by its service to the schools. An organization ought not be so doctrinaire that individuals stifle diversity by a desire to have everyone marching to the same excellence drummer. The confusion enters when the participants receive standards for excellence that are too broad to have any meaning, but all of them know that they need to prove that their unit fits the billing. More often than not, I find faculty or administrators who will tell me behind closed doors that they do not believe their unit is excellent, but that in order to answer some bureaucratic form or compete for ever-decreasing grants of money, they have concocted reasons about why their group is first rate.

Similarly, individuals also encounter problems if they seek data that will answer all their dilemmas. Again, because of the lack of comparability, one often finds that individuals are able to buttress their cases with data, but the data are inevitably flawed, circumscribed by human interpretation that seeks to prove whatever point the proponent desires. "How can you argue that I don't deserve a raise?" complains one professor. "I have more advisees than anyone else," and he offers the numbers to prove it. The individual's counterpart responds, "I have published more than anyone else in the department. Here are my articles." The problem, of course, is that simply knowing that someone advises 100 students says nothing about the quality of advising. If an individual advises 100 students and never meets with them, but someone else advises 20 students and meets with each student twice a semester, who is the better adviser? If a professor wrote six articles and none of them were refereed, and a colleague wrote two articles that were refereed, who was more productive?

In the first case, the answer is simple. The professor who never meets his 100 advisees is not the better adviser. However, the professor who meets 20 advisees may be doing a great job, but the department chair still needs the person to increase his or her load. In the second case, if the institution's emphasis is on generating knowledge to the public, then perhaps the individual who published six nonrefereed articles is more productive than the other professor who published only two, albeit in refereed journals.

Four data components, then, play a role in defining how good an organization is. *Context* is important because it enables individuals to understand specific constraints, possibilities, and histories. *Institutional values* help define excellence insofar as they circumscribe what the academic community defines as important, worthwhile activities. *Cultural facts* enable the organization's participants to decide on what basis they might make their judgements. The kind of information an individual provides over a specific time frame of necessity fosters an understanding of excellence based on the stated culture of the organization.

The fourth evaluative leg is *comparative*. What are one's colleagues doing? Academe is run by informal and ongoing assessments. A department at one institution is "hot" one day, and not the next; a dean has done an excellent job at one place and her counterpart at another place has not. If an organization wants standards of criteria, then comparability against their colleagues in other environments also aids in understanding how to define excellence and can help generate new ideas. Comparative data enable self-reflective judgments about how they are doing not because they need to mimic what others do, but in large part because it is a mirror of themselves.

Indeed, even to whom they choose to compare themselves says something. External definitions of excellence may not be in sync with how they define excellence. The comprehensive university that has actively decided it will not mimic research universities and instead wants to strengthen and develop new ways to work in the local community would not want its departments to make comparisons to major research universities; instead, the comprehensive university will seek other like-minded institutions that have sought a different path. Such information is doubly helpful. On the one hand, they make explicit their difference and celebrate it; on the other hand, they find organizations that seek a different path so that they are able to learn from one another.

Contexts, values, facts, and comparisons, then, form a schema upon which to base collective decisions. The schema also needs to be conveyed in a way that is simple, comprehensible, and attainable. Here is a partial hypothetical framework that might be used for a department:

We have decided to focus on two of the four goals of the university: community involvement and undergraduate education. Every professor spends no fewer than 5 hours a week working in local schools. We have developed five general education courses in a way that ensure that all senior faculty teach at least one section a year of a course that has as part of its requirement a service component where students deal with inner-city problems.

The faculty has the third highest publication rate in refereed journals of all related departments in the country. Our decision to involve ourselves in the problems of the local community has led to an award for innovative excellence and a television series on public television.

Granted, comments such as the one above are only part of an evaluative response, but they also speak to the kind of work the group values, and what the group is doing to achieve it.

Time Frames and Goals: The Short Term

A second way to evaluate high performance is to examine whether the organization's participants have met their goals. Indeed, organizations in disarray frequently have no goals. Those with attention deficit disorder have several goals over the course of a year and achieve none of them, skipping from one to the next. Too frequently when I ask a dean, department chair, or senior administrator what he or she hopes to accomplish in the next year or two, he or she is unable to articulate any clear response other than to say, "Make it through the year." I am equally troubled when I find the individual can provide a clear sense of what he or she hopes to accomplish, but faculty within the administrator's purview cannot describe organizational goals. Goals need to be articulated and shared in a reengineered organization. The idea that an elite group of individuals sets the direction and everyone else will simply follow is outdated and unhelpful. In today's academic environment, the successful organization needs individuals who buy into what the organization is attempting to do. Turbulent environments that create perilous fiscal times necessitate a shared understanding of what the organization is about and where the individuals want to go; at the same time, one ought not to expect unanimity. As I mentioned earlier, if a college or university must rely on consensus to make a decision, then it will be doomed to the status quo.

All units need clear short-term goals that one can articulate to external audiences, be it one's dean, a president, or a board of examiners. The hiring of a new professor or the installation of computers in every classroom that is unattached to any strategic plan is not the kind of goal I am suggesting. Rather, postsecondary institutions need to be able to articulate how they will perform better tomorrow than today, based on their overall vision of themselves. Sure, they want to capitalize on opportunities that arise out of nowhere. If a donor walked into someone's office and suggested a gift to renovate a building without any strings attached, the leader would be foolhardy to say, "That's not my goal this year, come back at a later date." I am not suggesting a rigid managerial line that is unable to adapt to changing needs and opportunities. On the other hand, crisis management is foolhardy if an organization's participants have no structured plan about where they want to go, how long it will take, how they want to get there, and how they are able to tell themselves and others how they know if they are getting there.

Individuals also need to be held accountable. The statement above about the department that works in the local community and has re-vamped its undergraduate curriculum may be well and good. However, if the same department also said that it intended to increase revenue by implementing an active recruiting program and in the space of a year made no discernable progress, then individuals in line positions would need to understand why and make needed changes. Goals are created not as perfunctory artifacts to please external audiences, but as markers about what the collective hopes to accomplish over a specific time frame.

Goals derive from the mission. I noted in the previous chapter that a mission needs to set direction, that it cannot be simply a visionary statement unconnected to the real world. The planning processes a leader puts into place (discussed in Chapter 2) lead, then, toward specific goals units intend to achieve.

Significant Goals: The Long Term

I have just finished saying that high-performing organizations need to have discrete indicators within finite, short-range time frames upon which individuals are able to evaluate performance. Now I will suggest, if not an opposing point, at least an idea that seems on a different tangent: the need for grand goals.

In a book about the successful habits of visionary companies, James Collins and Jerry Porras (1994) have called a commitment to daunting challenges "big, hairy, audacious goals (BHAGs)." They define BHAGs in this manner:

> A BHAG engages people—it reaches out and grabs them in the gut. It is tangible, energizing, highly focused. People "get it" right away; it takes little or no explanation. (p. 94)

Collins and Porras use as examples, among others, President John F. Kennedy's challenge to put someone on the moon by the end of the decade, and Sam Walton's goal to double the size of his company within 4 years. Their point is that as they investigated successful companies of the 20th century, what they discovered again and again was a commitment to BHAGs—risky goals that set the company on a path to outpace and distinguish itself from the competition, or possibly to miserably fail.

A trip to the moon or doubling the size of a for-profit business is certainly understandable as a significant, dramatic goal, but what kind of ventures are possible for a college or university? Why would such goals even be desirable? If an organization's participants want them, what are the risks and barriers to achieving them?

I have argued elsewhere for the importance of "anchoring ideologies" (Tierney, 1989). Ideologies are what individuals use to put the institution's mission into practice. Since I wrote that phrase, the need for a sense of what a college or university is about has grown. Fragmentation and disintegration of postmodern academic life have increased, not lessened. On the one hand, technology has enabled individuals to become more independent; on the other, the hyperprivatization and the concomitant withdrawal from the public domain has decreased any sense of understanding of the common good. Significant, hard-to-achieve goals move institutions away from minimalist survival techniques and toward a sense of identity and commonality across groups and interests.

Long-term goals, as anchoring ideologies, enact what the mission espouses. Individuals need an organizational identity in order to give meaning and affiliation to the work they undertake; such meaning and affiliation help create organizational commitment. At a time when resources are limited and human capital is essential, convening a sense of what the organization is about in concrete, bona fide ways, helps stimulate passion for one's work. Individuals also need to be able to communicate clearly to external constituencies how they are different from everyone else and why what they do is important to themselves and to others. And, of course, significant goals create the possibility of significant results.

When I visit campuses and find that institutions lack large goals, I often find a comparable inability among their leadership to think in broad schemes about where they want to go and how they want to get there. Individuals come to work, do their jobs, and go home. If the environment is not creating too many problems for them and the organization is stable, then who ought to complain if short-term goals are met, bills are paid, and students are happy?

The problem is that we all have entered a world in which organizational life will not be stable; the inability of an organization's participants to position themselves about where they want to go will affect both their destination and their immediate goals. Broad goals, those that evoke a gasp when someone mentions them, enable individuals to speak collectively about what they want tomorrow, and as a consequence, who they are today. Without such goals, the mission is too easily put aside and forgotten, something to be trotted out at appropriate moments but otherwise ignored.

Destinations and numbers are easy targets. One understands automatically the drama involved when someone says, "We will go to the moon within 10 years," or "We will double the number of stores we have throughout the United States within 5 years." What is a similar challenge that might be made in academe? Capital campaigns offer similarly easy targets: "We will raise $1 billion over the next decade." But such numbers do not create a sense of organizational excitement because they generally do not stimulate individual or collective ownership, or provide a sense of where the organization is going. There's no drama. In effect, a college president is going to raise money; a lot of money. That's good, but not in any way, shape, or form is it inspiring.

I visited a school of education recently and asked individuals what was the driving theme in their school. "We haven't had those kinds of discussions," said the dean. "I've never thought about it," said a department chair. "What do you think?" "We teach, do research." "We're not into blue sky stuff," responded a third person. "We're getting into distance education," added another.

I have visited a small public state college with a general education curriculum not unlike so many curricula that populate college campuses, a Rube Goldberg contraption that is a result of political trade-offs and individual whims built over the last generation. No one could provide a coherent rationale of why they had the courses, and the students had no understanding of what general education meant except that x number of classes were required to graduate. Everyone agreed that the curriculum lacked excitement and was not intellectually challenging, but it met political needs; different departments got a share of the general education pie and met their enrollment goals. When I asked individuals why they could not develop a unique and compelling curriculum, I heard comments such as, "It would be too difficult," "We're not that kind of place," "It's not great, but it's also not broken, so why change?"

Comments such as these depress and worry me. I mentioned in the introduction that a redesigned organization, by definition, has a commitment to excellence. When individuals do not frame themselves in a manner that positions their organizations for excellence, they fall far short of reengineering's emphasis. An inability to conceptualize what they might do to create a unique program suggests that the status quo is fine. In effect, colleges are driving 20-year-old cars; they assume that because the cars get them back and forth to work every day, there is no need to change. True, I could still use my electric typewriter to write this manuscript, but my work is faster, better, and more thorough because of technological innovations. Rather than a commitment to the status quo, here is what I might hear in an organization committed to achieving high performance:

- We will create a service learning program that is a national model, generates external grants, and raises student learning by 40% within 5 years.

- We will focus on urban issues and play an active role in reducing crime and raising educational standards in public schools by 50%.

- We will develop a curriculum that focuses on collaborative learning and become the best program of its kind in the country.

- We will become known as the university with the most technologically sophisticated and academically sound distance learning program in the country within a decade.

- We will become one of the top five state institutions in generating external funding within 10 years.

A variety of observations arise with such comments. Each statement begins with a plural pronoun. Big, hairy, audacious goals in academe must arise not from the office of a single individual, but from the collective. As I noted in the discussion about leadership, however, one new role of the leader is to facilitate and stimulate such issues. The leader makes BHAGs possible through guidance, confidence, and persuasion. One risk attached to such goals is that leaders need to stay in their jobs and maintain their focus. It is impossible to have organizations attached to significant goals if the leaders play musical chairs every 3 years and seek new jobs. Significant goals are the opposite of attention deficit disorder. On one side is an organization that cannot maintain a focus on any goal even for a short time period, and on the other is an organization that maintains a collective focus for a significant amount of time.

The goals need to derive from the mission of the organization. Presumably, the organization has an equally clear and compelling vision statement that enabled such goals to have been developed. A state college, for example, that stipulates in its mission statement that it serves working class students in the region and seeks to develop a sense of community involvement could obviously develop goals such as the one on service learning mentioned previously.

Each goal also has a time frame attached to it. How short-term and long-term goals interface is one facet of high performance. They do not always have to be attached to one another. Sometimes what one does in the immediate present will have little to do with the long-term goal. Short-term goals frequently may be more in the province of those involved in soft projects, whereas long-term goals may be those embedded in the structure. Although they do not need to be attached to one another, they also ought not be in contradiction. An institution should not, for example, have as a short-term goal a unit that needs significant funds for an international venture, if as a long-term goal they say nothing about international work and a great deal about local involvement. If both goals need fiscal support, the long-term goals need to drive short-term needs.

Significant goals also carry with them the risk of failure. A university is not modest when it says that it will develop the best service learning program or one of the five best programs in the country. If these goals are real and are believed, then they carry with them the possibility of failure. So be it.

If the organization is merely mouthing platitudes, "We will demand excellence," then it has nothing to lose, but little to gain. On the other hand, if it stakes its reputation on a particular venture, it may well find itself in trouble if it fails. Once again, I should emphasize the importance of the *we*. A collective vision enables the courage of the group to take risks not merely to make life interesting, but as a way to ensure organizational excellence and stimulate institutional desire.

Guidelines for Setting and Defining Goals

- Create a significant goal that needs no elaboration beyond one sentence. (It's a goal, not a statement.)
- Make sure it is significant. (A simple goal is obviously attainable; a significant one may not be.)
- Is a specific leader necessary to carry out the goal? (Significant goals should not be dependent on one person.)
- Once you have achieved the goal, what's next?
- Is the goal in sync with the organization's identity and mission?

Organizational Efficiency

I often find myself caught between two opposing camps when it comes to efficiency. Some individuals are devoted to efficiency and assume that if the task is completed on time then everything is fine. Others will argue that discussions of efficiency have no place in the academy and that those who desire efficiency are simply trying to impose Tayloristic principles on the academic enterprise.

A simple-minded adherence to efficiency without an overriding vision of why individuals in an organization need to be efficient is absurd. Obviously, when faculty ask their students to turn in their term papers, they expect more than their simply submitting the paper on time. Efficiency from this perspective becomes an end in itself, rather than a means to the realization of short- and long-term goals that support the organization's mission. However, efficiency of time, resources, and processes, is essential in both economically tight fiscal periods, and when an organization's participants want to achieve high performance. Colleges and universities of the 21st century will face both challenges: scarce resources and a desire to set high goals. Accordingly, efficiency is one other indicator that helps gauge whether an organization is actually reengineering and serious about reaching high performance.

What I look for in an organization committed to high performance is not simply a devotion to deadlines, but an understanding of why they want to meet those deadlines. If individuals know why they are doing what they are doing, then they need to consider the processes they use to reach their goals. The areas of analysis are time, money, and processes.

Short-term and long-term goals need to define the time frame in which we will conduct our work. Time frames are essential to ensure that we are working in a manner that enables us to move forward without slack time; time frames also prevent our working within such a short time frame that the achievement of the goal is impossible. In writing this, I feel that I am stating the obvious, except that I repeatedly encounter individuals and groups that have taken on tasks without having given any thought whatsoever about how long it will take or how fast they should move. "When do you hope to finish?" I will ask. "When we're done," I will hear. When individuals set temporal goals they are then able to work backward from them and plot out what needs to be done and where. They are able to outline tasks via the time frame.

Money is a similar matter. I am often surprised that when I ask someone how much he or she thinks a task will cost, I receive a shrug of the shoulders. At the same time, I am aware that we often cannot calculate costs down to the penny. When I submit budgets for grant proposals I may not be able to figure with precision the cost of airfare for a trip 3 years ahead, but I am able to calculate a rough estimate, and my foundation officers are equally adept at figuring out where someone has padded the budget. Inefficiency of fiscal resources cannot be overlooked, even if the group achieve their goals. That is, a college's participants may say that they intend to increase enrollment by 25% within 2 years, and they may achieve it. But if they spend 50% more than was necessary due to lack of efficiency, then the congratulations will be muted. Project, economize, and monitor expenses constantly. Money matters should not be left to the financial side of the house. I am not saying that everyone must become accountants. I am suggesting that a widespread understanding of costs increases the likelihood that the organization's participants will use their resources more efficiently.

The final area of efficiency deals with organizational processes. In large part, proponents of total quality management (TQM) have concerned themselves with the streamlining of procedures; in general, I agree with that as an objective. Comparing one's self to others, as I noted earlier, is akin to benchmarking, for example. But I did not write that the work of TQM is a *goal*; I wrote *objective*. TQM is insufficient without underlying philosophies and goals to give it purpose and direction. Efficiency for efficiency's sake is a waste of effort and may actually be counterproductive. However, anyone in academe can point out absurd administrative processes that can be improved upon.

For example, three different offices on campus ask me to submit (in three different formats) my publications over the last year. For a student to be admitted to my program, the candidate must get papers signed from six different offices. The paperwork involved for me to get reimbursed for a trip to a conference takes longer at my own institution than it does when I submit a simultaneous reimbursement request to a professional organization with which I work, even though the organization is 3,000 miles away. Each example illustrates a needless inefficiency.

Why a unit has such lethargic processes can often, though not always, be explained. When I undertake organizational audits, however, I am not interested in explanations about why something takes so long. I want to know how to improve it. When people's time is consumed on administrative trivia, the organization is shortchanged because these valuable people could be performing other tasks in an effort to achieve the goals the organization has elaborated. In a reengineered organization, all individuals are valuable.

Strategic Engagement: The Commitments

At the outset of the book, I listed five commitments: to community, academic freedom, access and equity, excellence and integrity, and inquiry. I have touched on some of these topics by way of other performance indicators. Significant goals pertain to a commitment to excellence, for example. However, infused throughout the other performance indicators needs to be a concern for the commitments. A college or university without an active, viable community that seeks to foster and extend academic freedom and inquiry to the community's members, and to educate the broad citizenry, is not a high performance academic organization.

In visits to college campuses I look for such indicators as defined by the institution's participants. Haworth and Conrad (1997) have given a name to such action by calling it *engagement theory*. They note:

> High-quality programs are those in which students, faculty, and administrators engage in mutually supportive teaching and learning: students invest in teaching as well as learning, and faculty and administrators invest in learning as well as teaching. Moreover, faculty and administrators invite alumni and employers of graduates to participate in their programs. In short, the theory accentuates the dual roles that invested participants play in constructing and sustaining programs of high quality. (p. 27)

Active governance and participation by the faculty, for example, is not merely a list of rules and procedures but the ongoing full engagement of faculty and administrators in the governance of the institution. Governance of this sort is an example of an engaged campus. Similarly, a devotion to academic freedom and inquiry gets played out in any number of ways, but primarily through discussions with faculty about their impressions of what they teach and research, how they teach, and infringements they may feel that are placed upon them.

I raise such issues here because when one speaks of excellence, high performance, and reengineering, one cannot overlook fundamental principles of what it means to be an engaged academic organization. Consider, for example, indicators that might be built around the idea of the commitments, so that the organization's participants would be able to assess whether they actually are involved in a high performance community. Here is a list of 13 culled from previous research I have done on different campuses:

1. A diverse outreach plan exists that encourages students from multiple racial and class backgrounds to apply.

2. A specific affirmative action plan grounds hiring policy.

3. A religious institution has a curriculum that focuses on its espoused beliefs.

4. A small college decides to emphasize collaborative learning, they develop learning communities of students and faculty, and the reward structure honors involvement in such communities.

5. A large private institution institutes a non-discrimination clause that includes gays and lesbians and then adopts a domestic partner policy.

6. A president points out that teaching is essential and teaches a class every semester.

7. Senior faculty offer first-year or introductory seminars.

8. The community holds weekly services that everyone attends.

9. Faculty commonly have interactions with students beyond the classroom.

10. Faculty and students are active in the community.

11. Local citizens are frequently seen on campus.

12. Governance committees exist in which students are actively involved.

13. Faculty sit on the Board of Trustees.

Examples such as these need to be noted with two caveats. First, not every example ought to apply to every institution. Individuals build engagement by dialogue within the organization. Second, the examples need to be *real* rather than merely lists that administrators or faculty use to fool one or another audience, such as accreditation agencies, other departments, or state higher education boards. All too often individuals create ways to portray themselves as excellent, so that they do not have to be excellent. Individuals snow people with data, but do not live engagement. What one needs is not merely a list of abstract figures on a page, but a sense of how these ideas develop the core beliefs of the organization and encourage change.

In a similar vein, Collins and Porras (1994) point out, "If you are involved in building and managing an organization, the single most important point to take away . . . is the critical importance of creating tangible mechanisms aligned to preserve the core and stimulate progress" (p. 89). In the words employed here, their "core" are my "commitments." An organization's participants ought not take such commitments lightly, or assume that such issues are intellectual niceties that individuals do not have time for as they create long- and short-term goals. If they do not nurture and foster the basic commitments, then all other issues are hollow and without meaning. The challenge is to develop a strategy that enables individuals to comprehend and make manifest what many see as fuzzy issues, such as community, intellectual freedom, and multiculturalism.

Conclusion

If I return to the start of this chapter and apply what has been discussed here, how might I respond to my brother's desire for a "bottom line," our colleague who spends time in the library without any results, or the provost who places a school in crisis management but seems to keep shifting focus? In one way or another, I have suggested that attention deficit disorder in organizations, although perhaps not the only cause of the problem, certainly is a significant part of it. An organization's participants are too often hyperactive; they jump from one issue to another, with the result that they remain wedded to the status quo.

I may never be able to respond to my brother in terms as simple as those with which he responded to me. However, I could certainly point out key parameters of organizational excellence if I raised the following summary questions and topics based on what I have outlined.

1. Do we have a culture that fosters ongoing, reflective assessment?
2. What do we want to accomplish?
3. What is the time frame and cost?
4. What significant task do we want to aim for?
5. Define the anchoring ideology of the institution (in a language that your parents will understand).
6. What facts do we agree are important indicators of accomplishment and excellence?
7. Who is our competition and how do we stack up?
8. What are the indicators of efficiency?
9. Outline our plan for strategic engagement with the organization's commitments.

The ongoing analysis of these issues will not ensure high performance, but it sets the stage for being able to discern where an organization's participants have succeeded and where they need to continue to improve. If these are organizational preconditions to high performance, then what we now need to consider are specific definitions we might use to define faculty performance. To this we now turn.

4

Faculty Productivity and Organizational Culture

When a man decides to do something he must go all the way, but he must take responsibility for what he does. No matter what he does, he must know first why he is doing it.

—Carlos Castañeda, *Journey to Ixtlan*

In academic circles there has been a great deal of discussion over the last decade about the importance of one's *standpoint* (Collins, 1991). The idea that who one is helps define what she or he says, in large part is a result of feminist and Black thought and a critique of how White, male social scientists largely overlooked women's and minority issues because of their male and Eurocentric standpoint. One might certainly quarrel with such a sweeping assertion; surely not every topic in social science is circumscribed by issues of gender or race. However, standpoint epistemology has made social scientists aware of the importance of one's background in authoring texts.

I raise this point in a chapter on faculty productivity in large part because of the contentiousness that surrounds discussions about faculty roles and rewards. People are variously labeled in ways that do not occur in other topical areas surrounding academe. When authors write about organizational culture or responsibility-centered budgeting, for example, readers most often deal with the strengths and weaknesses of their ideas irrespective of their personal characteristics. Issues surrounding faculty life are different. Someone will point out that a critic of tenure reform is a member of the American Association of University Professors (AAUP).

The comment takes on the ring of George Bush accusing Michael Dukakis of being a "card-carrying member of the American Civil Liberties Union" (ACLU), as if membership in such an organization were a sin. A vocal advocate for tenure reform will have pointed out that he is a tenured full professor at Harvard University; one need not be a deconstructionist to understand the general drift. How dare someone with tenure speak against it? An administrator who suggests a new way to deal with post-tenure review will discover that she "has sold out"; when she was a faculty member, she never would have suggested such an idea. One's standpoint does indeed mark one's self.

So let it be known: I am gay, politically on the left, White, a tenured faculty member at a research university, a card-carrying member of the AAUP, and a vocal advocate for reform. I raise these issues because they help define my own standpoint and also in part relate to why we have tenure and how I think of academic life. Tenure came about to ensure that individuals could investigate different areas of inquiry without fear of retribution or loss of their jobs. Certainly one's political affiliation and sexual orientation have at different times and at different institutions during this century been cause for dismissal. Tenure, then, is a protection that one would expect someone on the left who is gay to support. Similarly, I am a faculty member and I support the AAUP. Again, one ought to expect someone with such credentials to speak in defense of tenure. I will.

However, I also will argue here that we need to reform the roles, responsibilities, and rewards of faculty if we intend to achieve high performance in a reengineered organization. Reform does not mean the abolition of tenure. Indeed, the etymology of *reform* is "convert into another and a better form; improvement; radical change for the better" (Onions, 1966, p. 750). It is with such a meaning that I discuss faculty productivity.

This chapter is divided into three parts. I first discuss previous definitions of productivity and raise my own concerns with them; I then suggest how a redesigned organization might think about faculty productivity. I conclude the chapter by discussing how we might go about implementing changes aimed at reform.

Defining Productivity

A curiosity exists not only with our desire to know the standpoint of the discussant about faculty productivity, but also with the language used about the topic. Perhaps more than in any other occupation, academic life is framed by an overwhelming attention to the language used in constructing one's arguments. The professorate, whether in biology, engineering, or law, is trained in the art of critique. Faculty read articles, participate in oral examinations, and critique colleagues' presentations with an eye toward finding the flaws in one another's arguments. Such a concern spills over into the daily lives and into the governance of the institution.

Loose language, imprecise words in a document, or lack of specificity in a text are sure to stymie, if not destroy, a change effort. How to respond?

Because faculty governance is often cumbersome, and since individuals frequently have such a seeming obsession with wording, one response is where administrators throw up their hands and try to figure out ways to circumvent the faculty. As I noted in the Introduction, organizational life cannot be governed by cookbook solutions or recipes for decision-making. Obviously, at some point administrators can work around the faculty and nurture an idea to fruition. The ability to do so often pertains to the degree of trust and goodwill, or fear and animosity, that administrators and faculty have created. Ultimately, trying to avoid faculty governance and constantly doing end runs around the professorate is a mistake. High performance and reengineering demand involvement and active engagement, not the blind acceptance of centralized decisions which the faculty have played no part in developing.

A second response is to assume that the faculty do not understand the issues, and that if they did, they would agree with administrators. Such an assumption can be helpful and often leads to successful results. However, more often than not, efforts at educating the faculty are short-sighted if they do not also involve other actions. The scientific method may no longer hold prominence in academia, but by and large, faculty work from logical assumptions and causal models. When an administration states that an enrollment crisis exists and they desire to close four departments, faculty balk.

The art of administration involves being able to help create organizational futures; such futures are not a causal chain of events. Solutions depend, in large part, on a specific view of the world that the organization's participants have chosen. A cultural view of the organization assumes that the world is socially constructed; individuals help create their reality. Thus, decision making is infused with multiple options, so that frequently faculty and administrators do not have to make one specific decision.

Presenting a problem may help educate a populace about what they confront, but it may do little to convince that populace about the solution that has been proposed. What faculty frequently see happen is that an administration outlines the fiscal dilemmas that confront the institution, and then they propose closing some departments. Such a proposal is a non sequitur to professors who are thinking causally about "if x, then y." "Why close departments," wonder the faculty, "if we are in an enrollment crisis?"

Convincing the faculty of particular views of the world, and how to deal with those views, is usually unsuccessful when the college or university is in a crisis or has a piece of legislation that needs to be enacted. Again, dialogue ought to occur over a long period of time with multiple groups, rather than as a firefighter trying to put out a fire. Where faculty have been nurtured over time, when a crisis occurs the faculty are prepared and educated to deal with the problem. Recalling my notions of the new face of leadership in Chapter 2, reengineering deals with discussion, persuasion, and open communication, behaviors unfamiliar to those versed in centralized, hierarchical arrangements where information was not distributed as it is today.

Furthermore, only a small group of faculty have an active interest in governance. One college president commented that he agrees with engaging faculty in dialogue, but that faculty are often like students who do not do their homework all term. Their teacher has the unenviable task of trying to help the individual prepare for the final exam. Faculty have other issues to deal with such as their research and teaching, so that often they will not pay attention to governance issues until a crisis erupts. The challenge is to figure out how to utilize multiple groups, such as deans, department chairs, and senates to educate one another, and how to capitalize on the new technology to inform in constant, rather than stopgap fashion. Again, the importance of a cohesive mission and culture rises as central.

Although educating the faculty is important and useful, a third way to create the conditions for change so that faculty are on board with administrative efforts is equally necessary. Pay attention to the language used and the manner in which individuals communicate. *Productivity* makes faculty decidedly uncomfortable. Indeed, much of the language surrounding this whole debate seems framed in a way to inflame passions rather than calm them. At one institution that has instituted a form of post-tenure review a faculty member commented, "They [other faculty] went along to the ghetto [post-tenure review] because they were afraid if they didn't they'd be shuttled off to the death camp." Another person at a different institution where changes to the tenure code had been proposed added, "They [administrators] are giving us the shovels to dig our own graves once they've gassed us with their policies." I have heard productivity proponents speak of faculty as "dead wood," "senile," "immature," "people who couldn't get a job in real life," and "the major cause of all that's wrong around here."

I find such language retrogressive. I am not Jewish, but I nevertheless find it offensive that discussions about tenure reform are in any way compared to what happened to Jews during the Holocaust. I advocate reform, but we delude ourselves if we think we are going to create change by lobbing linguistic hand grenades at faculty or administrators and proclaiming that they are the root of all of academe's problems.

Change agents need to pay attention to language and how to communicate with one another. Such individuals need not only to educate the faculty but also also to appreciate and understand the cultural perspective, standpoint, and interpretation of groups different from their own. In order to concentrate on language, here are four common definitions of productivity.

1. "Productivity refers to the way in which a firm transforms inputs (e.g., labor and capital) into outputs." (Layzell, 1996, p. 269)

2. "Learning productivity relates the input of faculty and staff not to enrollments or to courses taught or to credit or classroom hours assigned, but to learning (i.e., the demonstrated mastery of a defined body of knowledge or skills)." (Johnstone, 1996, p. 2)

3. "[Productivity] will refer to an increase in educational outcomes (for example, more students served, improved instructional outcomes, a more valued mix of services) relative to costs, or lower costs for a given set of educational outcomes." (Levin, 1991, p. 242)

4. "The economist sees productivity as the ratio of outputs to inputs, [and] faculty focus mainly on the fraction's numerator." (Massy & Wilger, 1995, p. 20)

Now I offer representative quotes from interviews I have done with faculty about how they define productivity when queried.

1. "I don't think of it that way. I look at if someone produces sound work, has high standards for his students, is a good citizen around here. That kind of thing."

2. "If you ask me if Professor [Jones] is productive, I'm likely to say yes if he publishes a lot."

3. "A productive professor is someone who is a good teacher, helps his students learn, inspires them."

4. "Productivity has to do with the contribution you make to the field, to the profession, by what you do—teach, work in the lab."

5. "Am I productive? I guess I'd say yes because I write a lot, but I don't know really, because I work all the time. Doesn't productivity have something to do with efficiency, time on task? I don't think you can think of academic life that way. It's a calling."

6. "Productivity is a stupid word to use when you talk about teaching. Machine workers are productive, or an economy can be productive. What I do in the classroom has less to do with productivity and more to do with quality."

What might one interpret from these differing views of productivity? Administrators might throw up their hands and see whether they can impose tighter measures on faculty to ensure that they adhere to a more standard definition of productivity. As I mentioned, however, such attempts eventually run into brick walls, and reengineering demands participation, not administrative fiat.

Alternatively, if it were possible to explain how faculty work might be thought of as inputs and outputs, faculty would be better able to understand productivity. Such a comment, however, assumes that faculty see their lives and academic life in the same way that those who propose productivity measures do, and that the use of such language will improve the institution.

And the way to cope with diverse perceptions of productivity is to understand the perspective of multiple constituencies. Surely the use of a word or phrase is not the organization's end goal; rather, the goals ought to be about achieving the mission statement of the institution. If convincing faculty of an idea, rather than a word, becomes important, different questions arise. Why has productivity become an issue? Why are individuals concerned about defining faculty productivity? How do faculty respond to the problems? The answers revolve around five interrelated issues.

Fiscal Shortfalls

Institutions are in fiscal crisis; expenditures outstrip income. Sources of income, such as external grants, the federal and state governments, are declining. Colleges and universities need to reduce their expenditures. Well over half of an institution's costs go to salaries. Because most of those salaries are for faculty, and in many places upward of 60% of the faculty are tenured, the institution has fixed costs that are impossible to change. If faculty are productive, then such a percentage is not a problem. The twin assumptions, then, are that (1) those in academe must determine if faculty are productive, and that (2) not all faculty will be deemed productive.

Dead Wood

The argument is that postsecondary organizations have a group of people who are not productive. Business and industry have a ready-made way to deal with colleagues who are no longer productive. Those in academe are not even able to define faculty as unproductive because they lack the terminology.

Teaching Versus Research

A common complaint has been that faculty like to do research at the expense of teaching. A system that does not define productivity supposedly allows individuals to do whatever they want. If those in higher education defined productivity so that teaching was more prominent, they would then be able to reorient faculty work.

Maintaining the Status Quo

Technology is changing life so rapidly that postsecondary institutions need new definitions of productivity that replace what one currently thinks a productive faculty member does. Virtual universities, entire degree programs awarded through distance learning, and electronic publishing venues create a dramatically different framework for faculty roles and responsibilities. Unless those in higher education comprehend what the productive faculty member of tomorrow should do, colleges and universities will be unable to make the possibility of tomorrow a reality.

Tenure

Discussing tenure uncovers a curious dilemma with tautological reasoning. Productivity and tenure are linked as joint issues where tenure is asserted to be the framework that makes productivity less likely. Eliminate tenure and colleges and universities will become more productive. Define productivity and academics might be able to eliminate, or at least confine, tenure. The assumption is that tenure is the structure that does not allow productivity to be defined.

Conversely, academics can define productivity, argue some, but because of tenure all of the problems remain. Costs are fixed. Dead wood cannot be fired. Faculty can do whatever they want. If those in colleges and universities are able to determine productivity, however, then perhaps they will lessen the stranglehold that an outmoded concept such as tenure has on the academy.

The responses to these concerns have been swift and predictable (primarily from tenured faculty who are members of AAUP). Nowhere in the list of problems is there any mention of the need to protect academic freedom, a central premise of the institution. The problem of dead wood, however real, is minuscule. No research exists that a college or university has more dead wood than any other organization, and there is much anecdotal evidence that the broad majority of faculty work harder, as defined by time on task, than their counterparts in business and industry. Fiscal shortfalls are indeed a problem, but that is not because of faculty salaries; wages, unlike tuition, have not kept pace with inflation over the last decade. Productivity assumes that faculty work for monetary profit. If that were the case, many professors would be making much more money outside of academia. Although the evaluative system of faculty is not perfect, few businesses spend as much time deliberating over the hiring of an individual. Even fewer organizations have as rigorous a review of candidates as colleges and universities when they evaluate assistant professors who come up for promotion and tenure.

The result of this kind of back and forth has been largely a standoff. External constituencies, such as state legislators, or boards of trustees who come mainly from business and industry, perceive the faculty to be intransigent and unable to accept that dramatic changes are needed. Faculty believe they are not understood, at the least, and, at worst, that there is a plot to destroy academic freedom and intellectual life. Administrators often feel trapped between faculty and external constituencies. Changes need to occur. Faculty do have a point here and there, but so do those who advocate change.

How, then, do we approach the problem of productivity? What is the problem that we are trying to solve? To answer these questions it will be helpful to understand three issues: (1) faculty employment profiles at the end of the 20th century; (2) proposed solutions; and (3) how productivity fits within an academic culture.

Employment Profiles

Obviously, defining the productivity of a faculty member requires combining multiple criteria that are both extrinsic to and at the same time defined by the individual. Minimal standards of teaching excellence, for example, might be developed irrespective of who is teaching. Different expectations exist for a full professor than for his or her junior counterpart. Individuals might face a personal catastrophe during the course of a year that make them less effective. In such a case it is possible to contextualize understanding and decide that, given the circumstances, Professor X had a productive year.

A productive faculty member's work will be dramatically different depending on whether she or he teaches at a private research university, a comprehensive state university, or a community college. What one's colleagues expect from a professor of engineering will not be similar to the expectations of a classics professor. An organization's participants will have different criteria for a part-time professor versus a full-time faculty member. What they expect of someone on the tenure track may well differ from what they desire of someone off-track.

Although such comments are commonsensical, unfortunately colleges and universities have sought throughout this century to fit everyone into one mold when it comes to defining productivity. If community colleges are excluded, for example, all institutional types reward research over teaching (Tierney & Bensimon, 1996). Certainly a professor at a research university might publish more than her or his counterpart at a comprehensive university; however, when two individuals at the same institution are compared, we will discover that the individual who publishes more will receive a greater reward, as defined by salary increase and/or promotion.

The argument also seems to be focused on arguing over what to expect of tenure-line faculty when the fastest growing group in the professoriate are those who are off the tenure track (Gappa, 1996). Indeed, faculty and administrators frequently laud on the one hand the amount of time spent hiring and evaluating a tenure-line professor, but on the other hand have a cavalier attitude toward how they hire and evaluate a part-time or nontenure-track faculty member. One wonders why one would spend so much time defining the productivity of a tenure-track individual who works in one office and virtually none on her colleague who works full-time, but is not tenure line. Indeed, given the rise in nontenure-line positions, a case might be made that more effort should be spent in evaluating their productivity in so far as most of our traditional criteria (hiring, promotion and tenure guidelines) are absent.

Judith Gappa (1996) has pointed out the following:

- Two thirds of all faculty are full-time.
- Three fourths of all full-time faculty are tenure track.
- One half of all faculty in all institutions are not on the tenure track.
- Recent full-time faculty hires over the last 5 years reveal an increasing trend toward hiring nontenure-track faculty.

The implications here are straightforward. Rightly or wrongly, institutions are moving toward hiring nontenure-track faculty in part-time and full-time positions. Evaluative criteria developed over this century have seen a drift toward a "research model": one's productivity gets measured in terms of research output rather than other criteria, such as teaching, service, or direct work in the community (Tierney, in press). But these criteria do not apply to nontenure-track faculty, and no other standards are being adopted. There is certainly no grand plan about how to proceed, so what is taking place are individualized institutional efforts at resolving the problems outlined previously. In what follows, I sketch what some of the major proposed solutions have been thus far.

Proposed Solutions to Analyzing Productivity

Contracts

Perhaps the most direct attack on tenure is the suggestion that colleges and universities move from a system based on tenure to one based on long-term contracts. An individual could be hired for a fixed period, perhaps 5 or 6 years, and would then go through the process of renewing his or her contract, not unlike a baseball player. Three assumptions underlie this approach.

First, an organization's participants would be able to periodically gauge the productivity of the individual to ensure that the professor still performs adequately. Second, productivity would be able to be located within a specific context. For example, the individual might be productive if judged by extraneous criteria, but unproductive with regard to the needs of the organization. Over time, the organization may decide it no longer needs a professor in art history, for example, but has a major need in accounting. It could then choose not to renew the art history professor's contract. And finally, productivity in some way needs to be defined in relation to institutional costs. Again, some will argue that it is counter-productive to carry an individual if the institution cannot afford such a commitment.

The argument based on these assumptions is that this tenure does not enable those in academe to gauge productivity over the faculty life span, while a contract system will enable them to define productivity. Criticism of this suggestion generally has little to do with productivity. Rather, what one hears is that tenure was instituted to protect academic freedom; to destroy tenure is to destroy academic freedom. A by-product of tenure is that colleges and universities have a quite productive faculty. They just cannot measure productivity in a way that is done in the business world.

Furthermore, critics of the proposal argue, the assumption that tenure is at fault is mistaken. If the criteria used to obtain tenure are tilted incorrectly (e.g., emphasizing research over teaching), then the faculty can change the criteria. If they do not have an accurate measurement of what faculty do after they receive tenure, then they can develop fair measures.

Productivity and Salary

A second option is to tie salary to productivity. Those individuals whom an organization's participants define as productive will get salary raises; those who are not productive will not receive raises. Obviously, the market comes into play. Imagine two individuals who are equally productive, but one teaches in classics and the other in business. The business professor can command a higher salary.

Many institutions already have this kind of system, but proponents suggest that colleges and universities need clearer criteria. That is, merit raises occur in many colleges and universities, but how to define productivity more often than not relies on the subjective judgment of a dean or provost. Other institutions, usually public state universities, decide that pay raises will be equal across the campus. The criticism of this procedure is that it rewards mediocrity. Why should someone receive a raise simply because everyone else receives one?

Although a system linking salary increases to productivity usually does not meet with the same objection that a move to a contract system does, concerns do exist. On the one hand, critics point out that unless the specific criteria by which one judges productivity are changed, many of the problems will not change. That is, if an organization simply clarifies how to judge a productive teacher but does not change the underlying structure, then they will simply have a clearer understanding of discrete activities (e.g., teaching), but still reward one undertaking over another.

On the other hand, some individuals charge that even using a word such as *productivity* and tying it to salary infringes on one's academic freedom. Faculty should be able to pursue what they want, argue the critics, and not be punished or judged as unproductive if they do not meet standardized criteria. From this perspective, faculty life is inherently productive, but one's work is so individualized that it defies this kind of analysis.

Post-Tenure Review

One way to deal with the problems mentioned above, such as dead wood and the status quo, is to institute a formalized post-tenure review system under which the organization's participants will be able to monitor an individual's progress. Unlike a contract system, post-tenure review does not replace tenure. The options are multiple. One possibility is that every individual is reviewed once every 3 years. If the individual receives a poor assessment then he or she might have an annual review. A second option is that all faculty have an annual review. A third option is that only those individuals who are deemed unproductive are reviewed.

Again, most criticism of this approach has more to do with the procedures than with any basic infringements on academic freedom. Because few institutions have instituted any systematic approach to post-tenure review, it has not been widely accepted. As faculty, they are not able to see the potential shortcomings or abuses of the system, so any meaningful changes usually have not taken place. Individuals also express concern about the cumbersome nature of the review. They point out how time-consuming a current tenure review is and wonder if it is worth the effort simply to deal with a microscopic percentage of the faculty known as "dead wood." Indeed, one hears that consuming faculty time in evaluative activities is counterproductive. It actually will make people less productive because they take time away from basic activities such as teaching and research. Similarly, some argue that a system designed to be punitive creates a climate of fear that gravitates against a productive workplace.

Productivity and Culture

Throughout this book, I have maintained the importance of the language if change agents want to see their ideas implemented. The words in an institution's mission are critical to how individuals see themselves. How a leader communicates goes a long way in defining an organization's reality. Language could not be more important when speaking about faculty life.

Productivity, as defined previously, has a harsh, shrill ring to it that presumably reduces faculty work to a series of managed activities that can and must be monitored and evaluated. The interpretation one frequently ascertains from discussions about productivity is that faculty are trying to get away with something, that they have a good life, and they do not want anyone to disturb it. The assumption is that there is a need for productivity measures to sanction individuals and to rid the organization of unproductive personnel.

Productivity, framed in this manner, has two fatal flaws. First, one cannot create long-term, dynamic change in an environment in which the organization seeks to scare or demean the general population. Fundamental change in an organization that relies on intellectuals occurs only when trust is widespread.

Second, the perception that faculty are lazy is simply incorrect. In previous research in which I interviewed close to 300 individuals specifically about their lives on the tenure track, I discovered faculty who put in remarkably long hours at relatively low pay (Tierney, 1997; Tierney & Bensimon, 1996). The faculty I interviewed frequently work weekday evenings and at least one day on weekends.

Individuals may not be undertaking tasks that others want them to perform, but that is a different matter. Perhaps some institutions should reorient what faculty do so that teaching or engaged work with the external community receives greater emphasis. To do this, however, requires a change in the reward structure, not by labeling individuals as unproductive. One ought not lay accusations at people's feet if they are undertaking tasks for which they are rewarded. Instead, the organization's participants ought to change the reward structure.

Furthermore, at no institution where I have spoken with faculty or administrators have I heard anyone say that dead wood is a significant problem. Certainly, each department or school has a war story about an individual whom everyone would judge as unproductive, but the problem is not pervasive. Rather, it can be handled on a case-by-case basis. I know of no company that does not have a problem with a small percentage of its workforce. Disaffected, unproductive employees are a constant source of concern, but one ought not paint everyone else with a broad brush stroke as unproductive, or at the least suspect.

To develop high performance in individuals, three broad challenges exist for the organization.

1. How to aid and support those individuals who are intrinsically high performers (perhaps 10% of the faculty)?
2. How to enable and encourage the broad middle to achieve high performance (perhaps 85% of the faculty)?
3. How to provide an environment so that those who are unproductive are able to change, improve, or rethink their roles (perhaps 5% of the faculty)?

Such questions help locate productivity within an organization's culture in a fundamentally different way from the previous concerns discussed up to this point. John Collier (1973), an anthropologist who spent his life working with Native Americans and their struggles over schooling, once wrote:

> I move forward in this writing, as I did in the field experience itself, seeking an educational definition that offers people, no matter how different from others, a productive place in the modern world. I write with conviction that not only are people and peoples inherently unique but that civilization is enriched and tempered by this diversified vitality. (1973, p. 6)

I resonate to the tone and substance of what Collier wrote. He works from a language of respect, strength, and conviction about individuals, groups, and productivity. How might an organization's participants apply Collier's words to the discussion?

He begins by saying, "*I move forward in this writing, as I did in the field experience itself . . . ,* " simply enough. Those individuals involved in academic change and appraisal may assume a similar mantle: We move forward in the creation of productivity guidelines, as we do in our daily work with one another.

He sought "*an educational definition that offers people, no matter how different from others, a productive place in the modern world.*" Collier seeks an *educational* definition. The implication is that multiple definitions exist, but when we speak of educational organizations and processes we are involved in something special. He also seeks a definition that *offers* people something. Consider how dramatically different a definition is that *offers* people rather than *demands* or *commands* people. Here we have an emphasis on a framework that places the onus on the organizational community rather than the individual. A definition that demands is one of oppression or imposed discipline or coercion; a definition that offers is one of encouragement.

As opposed to a unitary approach, Collier acknowledges that he wants a definition that allows individuals, "*no matter how different from others,*" to find a "*productive place.*" We then have an organizational schema in which multiple possibilities exist. Economists will grumble that Collier's use of "productive" is not what they mean. Precisely. He does not speak of inputs and outputs. Nevertheless, his language is one that befits an academic community, and it creates a schema that an organization's participants might employ to ensure high performance.

Collier compounds the problem for traditional economists: *"I write with conviction that not only are people and peoples inherently unique. . . ."* Again, his language, infused with hope, ought to find sustenance in our own institutions. We also ought to write with conviction, rather than cynicism or vindictiveness. If we want high performance we must be able to come to terms with defining the best in individuals, rather than seeking their weak points in order to expose them.

He concludes by speaking about the importance of such diversity and how civilization is *"enriched and tempered by this diversified vitality."* Those individuals in academe might write that organizations are similarly enriched and tempered. The struggle is how to enact such hopeful language. I appreciate that the accountant with the proverbial green eyeshade may be uncomfortable with discussions about productivity that begin with convictions, offer multiple opportunities for people, and place the emphasis on the community creating the conditions for high performance. An easier, albeit unsuccessful, way to go is to create productivity indices within the confines of one's office, publish them, and then watch to see who can and cannot reach the high bars that have been set.

I am suggesting that productivity in an academic community begins from dramatically different premises from the ones the discussion has taken us to at this point. Michael Katz (1987) has written that the ideal university

> should be a community of persons united by collective understand-
> ings, by common and communal goals, by bonds of reciprocal obliga-
> tion, and by a flow of sentiment which makes the preservation of the
> community an object of desire, not merely a matter of prudence or a
> command of duty. Community implies a form of social obligation
> governed by principles different from those operative in the market-
> place and the state. (p. 179)

From this perspective, productivity is not a bureaucratic search for indicators so that decision-makers are able to reward some and sanction others. If an academic community exists by way of bonds of "reciprocal obligation," then as faculty they might develop productivity indicators with two key goals in mind. First, productivity ought to be an ongoing activity that the organization's participants think about throughout an academic year. Simply stated, if individuals plant an orchard, the health and beauty of the fruit is not something determined by when the growers pick them, but by the processes they use to grow them and the care they demonstrate at nurturing them.

Second, as a member of the academic community, the individual also has an obligation to the community. His or her responsibility to teach to the best of his or her ability, for example, ought not be measured on an obscure chart that needs to be filled in for state agencies. Rather, the "bonds of affiliation" that the individual has with his or her colleagues ought to necessitate that everyone perform well for one another. Productivity is not a bureaucratic measure for individual excellence, but the vehicle that offers faculty particular rights and responsibilities.

Thus, if academe is a community in search of high performance, then individuals need to focus more centrally on how productivity is an ongoing developmental activity. The discussions move away from defining the problem as dead wood or how tenure is an impediment to change (Tierney, 1997). Instead, the organization's participants ought to focus their attention on improving the culture of faculty life by discussing in depth, honestly, concretely, and personally, how they as a faculty, and one's self as an individual, might improve. Productivity in this manner moves away from a culture of fear and retribution, and toward an understanding of how to achieve the diversity that Collier defined. The challenge is how to implement a climate for improvement.

Initiating and Maintaining Dialogues About Productivity

High performance organizations are those that have a supportive culture that demonstrates to one's colleagues that all individuals in the organization have obligations to one another. Rice (1996) and I (Tierney, 1993) previously have written about the present conditions in academe as making individuals feel isolated from one another and bereft of social community. How might the organization move toward a productive workplace? I present five ideas, and again provide a list of questions to ask.

Fear Versus Encouragement

From the viewpoint that I elaborated on employing the work of John Collier and Michael Katz, an organization's participants proceed in an environment in which they seek human development and potential rather than sanction. Discussions of ways to help faculty improve and develop enable them to create definable goals about how the individual and the unit might mutually support one another. Intellectual development becomes an undertaking, nurturing individuals rather than browbeating them into submission.

An analogy to teaching is appropriate. We have learned what makes for a productive learning environment. Classrooms in which teachers commonly use derogatory terms toward their students and have minimal standards, with the assumption that students are apt to fool around or are unable to achieve, are ineffective learning environments. The most productive classrooms are those that convey, in an ongoing manner, high standards in an atmosphere in which students are capable, intelligent, and welcome. Organizations need to apply the same idea in their relations with one another.

---

1. Is the discussion about evaluation and productivity framed in a positive manner? How do you know?

2. Are discussions about evaluation and productivity part of the common fabric, or do they occur only when crises occur and problems arise?

3. Do individuals have a clear sense of what is expected of them?

Professional and Communal Identity

Faculty need a sense of the kind of institution they reside in, and how it fosters the work they undertake. One of the problems in determining individual concerns versus collective needs is that the individual often has an unclear collective identity or none at all. Mission statements that derive from strategic plans are vague goals about excellence rather than specific measures about what they intend to do, so they are hard for faculty to identity with.

Faculty receive degrees from elite institutions in which they become socialized to the norms of academic life. The norms graduate students receive are those that research institutions convey, especially in undergraduate education, that research is important, teaching is secondary, and service is to be kept to a minimum. In this value system one finds community among one's professional colleagues who are scattered across the country. Individuals communicate with their colleagues once or twice a year at conferences, and increasingly, almost daily via electronic mail, fax, and teleconferences. Who needs the institution for community when its expectations are unclear and intellectual stimulation occurs elsewhere?

The vast majority of individuals, however, do not teach and work in research universities, even though they have been socialized by them. Individuals populate the postsecondary universe in community colleges, small institutions, and large comprehensive organizations where teaching ought to be given predominance, but the research culture has taken hold. Even those faculty in research universities might point out that the sense of intellectual, social, and emotional distance they feel from their institutional colleagues is not optimal, but that their professional colleagues elsewhere at least make life manageable. In effect, they are saying since they cannot find community on their campus, they will make it elsewhere.

---

1. Ask faculty if they can define in simple terms the mission of the institution.

2. Have faculty define how their school's or college's strategic plan fits the mission of the institution.

3. Have faculty explain how their own work dovetails with the strategic plans of their unit and institution.

4. Ask faculty, "When was the last time you had an *interesting* discussion with someone from another department on campus?"

Performance Contracts

In an earlier section I raised two issues that are relevant here. First, an organization's participants often do not evaluate the performance of nontenure-track faculty. Second, productivity is often tied to merit raises and little more. Performance contracts should be for all faculty. The organization develops a contract primarily as a way to enable individuals to set goals for themselves and to announce to the community how their work enhances the strategic plan and mission of the organization. As a by-product they will be able to reward those who are high performers and perhaps reconfigure contracts for those few who have not performed well. How might such an activity occur?

First, one's work may invariably change over the course of an academic year. A colleague may abruptly leave, and the individual may be asked to teach a course. Someone may invite a faculty member to participate in an edited book for which he or she had not planned. A performance contract should not be so constrictive that there is no room for capitalizing on such unforeseen opportunities.

However, the faculty also need to come to common agreement about how they define productivity. They frequently have general notions. At many research institutions, they say that one's work should be 40% teaching, 40% research, and 20% service. There is a need for greater specificity. Surveys that list a variety of undertakings so that the faculty member is able to summarize his or her work is one such possibility. A teaching portfolio is an example of another way to gauge productivity. The goal should be to develop an evaluative system that gives everyone a broad understanding of one's work; to aim for much greater specificity is most likely a waste of time. The work of the faculty is an intellectual undertaking and ultimately human judgment comes into play about how an individual performs.

However, once the organization's participants have standardized criteria that have been developed and approved by the faculty they have a form to gauge one's performance over the past 12 months. A performance contract then delineates what an individual intends to do over the next 12 months. Obviously, some contracts are simple and straightforward. An individual will list the number of courses he or she has planned, describe the research he or she intends, and list the committees on which he or she will participate. In some cases, however, an individual will have a record of conducting no research so one might think that the performance contract might incorporate more teaching to compensate lack of performance in the other area. If the expectation is that faculty will have a specific advising load and an individual does not meet the load, then the contract would specify how the individual intends to make up the work in another area.

In a community concerned with development and quality there is an obligation to outline where an individual intends to go, and how he or she intends to get there. The point is to ensure that all individuals have productive roles, that everyone is able to work to his or her highest capacity, and that the community supports the actions of what one another does. If a college or university develops performance contracts, then how to think of administration, and what we currently conceive of faculty roles and responsibilities, also shifts.

---

1. Is there an evaluative mechanism in place that is more than a pro forma document?

2. Is there active and diverse faculty involvement in the development and evaluation of faculty performance?

3. Is a performance contract in place that enables individuals to link future work with past performance?

The Dialogical Administrator

Although all administrators should be dialogical, I focus here more on mid-level administrators, particularly at the departmental and dean's level. I also accept the world as it is; soft projects are a goal to work toward and implement. For the time being, however, the vast majority of faculties reside in departments and divisions. In work I have done, I have found that newer faculty frequently define their universe as ending at the school or college level; anything beyond that level, unless they play extraordinary roles, takes on the shape of a foreign country.

Administrators need to be dialogical in two senses. First, they need to develop in administrators a sense that one of their main tasks is helping faculty fulfill the objectives they have set out for themselves. In this light, the work of a department chair is formative; discussion is ongoing, and centers on how the department might better enhance the quality of life for the individual.

The second task is summative. The department chair or dean needs to have frank, formal discussions about an individual's performance contract and rectify errors when they exist. In the study that Bensimon and I conducted of junior faculty, even for those on the tenure track we discovered feelings of drift and lack of clarity about what was expected of them (Tierney & Bensimon, 1996). Honest dialogue about expectations that confronts shortcomings, objectives, goals, and institutional needs in a straightforward manner offers dramatic opportunities for change.

I cannot emphasize enough the importance the organization needs to place on dialogue surrounding definitions of productivity. I also am not utopian. Any current administrator will recognize that 80% of the faculty will buy into what I have suggested, and 20% will tie the organization into knots. However difficult these dialogues may be, the key here is to stay focused. Unproductive individuals not only harm themselves but also create a depressed climate in organizations in which resources are limited. Individuals begin to wonder why they should work hard, if the fellow down the hall does not. Bonds of social obligation suggest that individuals have responsibilities to one another.

---

1. How often do you meet with your faculty?
2. How does the outcome of a performance review get resolved?
3. Is the process for review, disputes, and grievances, clearly shared and understood by everyone?

Faculty Responsibilities

I have noted how "tenured faculty who are in the AAUP" have approached changes from a frequently intransigent standpoint. They certainly have justification. If the tenor of the discussion is negative about one's work, then the professor may well expect that he or she will respond in kind. However, if the discussion needs to change from the administrative standpoint, then it also needs to change from a faculty perspective.

In a community in which responsibility is shared, the role of the collective is to develop a self-regarding culture in which all individuals are proactive, rather than reactive, to perceived and real problems that confront us. Thus, a key cultural response to the problems that confront academe is for faculty to develop solutions of their own, rather than merely defeat ill-conceived solutions of others. Rather than try to avoid faculty governance, I submit that the faculty need to use it as a key vehicle for redesigning the organization.

It is not helpful to add yet another meaningless activity on an already busy group. But if one assumes that teaching, learning, and research are important, then an organization's members need to build efficient ways to work with one another about how to improve one another's work and gauge individual and group productivity.

---

1. Define what it will take to create an effective faculty governance system.
2. What dissuades people from involvement, and what will it take to overcome the problems?
3. Does the faculty have an explicit sense of the responsibilities it has a group, and can it be articulated by all members?

Ultimately, this chapter may disappoint those who want specificity and exact measurement of one's work. I have suggested here why exactitude is unimportant. Productivity in an organization's culture is more concerned with ensuring that everyone is playing to the best of his or her ability and that all individuals are operating from the same plan, agreeing about the texture that they desire, and how they will interact with one another. Different musicians have different roles; a group's responsibilities are to one another, to the music, and to the audience. An organization has intrinsic and extrinsic definitions about how to judge an individual's playing. Optimally, the music is joyful and the musician's work is personally fulfilling and appreciated.

5

The Chiaroscuro of Reform*

Consequently: he who wants to have right and wrong,
Order without disorder,
Does not understand the principles
Of heaven and earth.
He does not know how
Things hang together.

—Chuang Tzu

One of the great revelations of the Renaissance was the interplay between light and dark in painting. The disposition of light and shade (*chiaro* = clear; *oscuro* = dark) enabled artists to contrast scenes of nature and society where the two were intermingled. Those of us involved in reengineering need to be postmodern chiaroscurists. Organizational life is filled with contrasts where the shade of one area heightens the coloring in another. All too often what academic managers have tried to do is create organizational palettes that blend colors into a coherent framework as if organizational life is a color-by-numbers undertaking. Scientific management and bureaucracy, for example, were attempts at organizing structures and people around the idea of uniformity rather than difference. Administrators felt the need to monitor employees. Time clocks, standardized production outputs, and centralized decision-making are examples of managerial attempts to do away with contrasts. They focused on making

---

*I am indebted to my colleague, Rollin Kent, for discussing this phrase with me.

organizational functions more routinized and efficient with the assumption that in doing so, better organizations developed. One color scheme fit all paintings.

In the late 20th century, we have made mild attempts around the edges of organizational life to allow different shades to enter the portrait. An organization might allow flextime so that not everyone must punch in at 9 and out at 5. Organizational units, rather than individuals, might be responsible for production levels, so employees can undertake a variety of tasks rather than routinized ones. Broader decision-making patterns exist today in even the most conservative of organizations. More individuals have access to information than ever before. Such facts are meager examples of attempts to take advantage of, rather than stifle, diversity. Nevertheless, organizational patterns and frameworks remain in place. Rather than getting out of the box, those involved in organizational change have simply rearranged a few features within the box. Such changes are little more than moving the chairs around on the *Titanic*. Faculty and administrators need ways to let go of their assumptions in their thinking and in organizational designs. Reform must deal with contrasts—with chiaroscuro.

One also runs risks with chiaroscuro. Contrasts of light and dark highlight difference rather than uniformity. If one carries the point to its logical conclusion one might see organizational units running in different directions, so that any sense of mission stressed in previous chapters will be obliterated. It is also possible to see the contrasts as obscurity at a time when an organization's participants need greater clarity. The metaphor that academe prides itself with is, more often than not, that of the shining light on the hill, a beacon for the search for truth. Surely chiaroscuro has no beacon of light; or if it does, it is set off by storm clouds.

However, those of us who will work in the postmodern organization need to deal with contrasts. Organizational redesign has more to do with working with differences, or organizing with differences, rather than trying to use broad brush strokes to eliminate them. Indeed, the assumption I have worked from is that only by coming to terms with these differences will an organization's participants be able to deal with the multitude of problems that confront them. And one does not deal with reform by tinkering around the edges with light and dark. The kind of suggestions I have proffered, such as soft projects, performance reviews, and decentralized leadership, pertain to a wholesale rethinking of what is meant by organization. Such changes are never easy. One may concoct the most brilliant plans in her or his head, but unless such dreams are made tangible and implemented, they are merely whimsical notions of what could have been, rather than what is. Accordingly, I discuss here the chiaroscuro of reform.

If an organization's participants accept what I have outlined up to this point, what are the initial steps that could be taken to implement fundamental changes in the organization? How do individuals work with chiaroscuro? If an organization frees people by decentralizing decision-making or emphasizing the importance of keeping organizational structures in flux, how do the organization's participants ensure that chaos does not overwhelm them, change is not stymied, and their goals are reached?

In what follows, I offer five topics that deal with these questions. As I will elaborate, each topic needs to be painted in chiaroscuro, and in doing so, any college or university of course runs risks and I will discuss them. However, not to focus on these topics is one sure way of failing at organizational redesign. The topics themselves, communication, incentives, power and control, information, and strategy are not new. The difference is how to utilize them in a reengineered organization.

Communication

One job I held as I worked my way through college in Boston was as a quasi-counselor at the Pine Street Inn, a home for homeless men, located in the red-light district of Boston. My job was to keep the peace; no easy task on cold winter days or hot summer afternoons when the cavern-like hall filled with close to 200 men of all racial and ethnic categories and whose ages ranged from 16 to 80-something. In the 1970s, some of the men were down on their luck, and some smoked marijuana, but the overwhelming majority had drinking problems. One of my tasks was to prevent anyone from entering the building with an alcoholic beverage. If I found someone who had a jug, I was to figure out how to get him to leave. Early on in my tenure at Pine Street, I found myself alone on a Sunday afternoon when one shift had left and the other shift had yet to arrive. Sure enough, two fellows walked in the building drunk and holding bottles. I also saw the director of the Pine Street Inn walk quietly into his office at the same time. I went back to him and asked him what I should do.

"Look, Tierney, you're new here. This is the way it works. Treat the men with respect. They have needs and you deal with them. Make decisions. Use your common sense."

His words stung, but rung true. Little did I realize that his advice not only would hold me in good stead at the Pine Street Inn for 3 years, but also would be valuable as a basis of management principles for how people should act in colleges and universities. These men were the kind of fellows we see one or two at a time on street corners asking for spare change. A common response is to keep our eyes down and walk by them, or roll up the car windows and lock the doors. I was to treat these men with respect and serve their needs. If a homeless shelter is able to serve its clientele in this manner, then one might think that a college or a university should be able to do the same. Sadly, more often than not, we do not.

I was a 19-year-old, and yet I was given the freedom to make decisions. Certainly, the administrators at the Pine Street Inn had elaborate formal and informal structures to help ensure that the staff accomplished their work and that they received help when needed. But the emphasis was on service. If the staff did not treat the individual with respect, then he or she was gone. When the staff made decisions the administration backed the staff so that in a very real sense the staff was able to exhibit leadership of the kind I discussed in Chapter 2. If the staff were unable to make decisions, or did not buy into the focus of the Inn, then they were let go. The same single focus should pertain to academic work in the vast majority of postsecondary institutions, but it is absent.

All too often, faculty, staff, and administrators in a college or university have no sense of whom they serve or what they do, other than meeting demands that someone else has placed upon them. The dean asks for workload sheets to be filled in, and the individual grudgingly does it. A prospective student calls up to ask for information about a particular program and is directed to three different offices before he gives up. A current student comes for an appointment with her professor and discovers the office locked and the secretary unaware of when the professor will return.

An initial challenge in a reengineered organization is to organize around customers rather than the functions listed on a job description. The use of the word *customer* is purposeful and upsetting, and underscores the first principle of the chiaroscuro of reform. To use a phrase my colleague, Ellen Chaffee, has employed, we must, "listen to the people we serve" (1998, p. 13).

Serving People

When a college or university's participants listen to those who use postsecondary education, they refocus energies in fundamental ways. Does the history professor teach the Renaissance or teach students? Does the secretary meet the needs of the students or the demands of his boss? Does the administrator create fiscal structures that make it easier for her to complete her end-of-month statements or structures that make it easier for individuals to get paid on time? One facile response is that such questions do not have to be trade-offs. Clearly, a professor needs to be an expert in the Renaissance if he or she is adequately to teach students, just as a secretary might meet student needs by completing work required by a superior. People certainly do not go out of their way to create a climate that is alien to their customers.

In a reengineered organization, however, the focus changes. The customer is not a by-product of the organization's actions. Rather, the customer frames the organization's actions. I initially had a visceral reaction against the use of the term *customer*. I tend to think of academe more like a religion than a business. The IBM Corporation has customers, while the Catholic Church has souls. Unlike a business, when students are done with their college education they do not own a palpable product such as a car or a microwave. Rather, they have improved themselves internally, their well-being, much as they might have by participating in religious services.

I also am not in any way advocating that academe's purpose be devalued so that those involved in academic life define academe's "product" as enabling the student to get a job. Certainly, most postsecondary institutions need to focus intensively on employment for their clientele. But at its best, a college education offers something much closer to what a church is supposed to provide, than what a business is supposed to do. Faculty and administrators help individuals grapple with difficult issues about life and death, and the meaning of life. They aid students in their quest to become productive citizens. To speak of such grand challenges in the language of customer relations runs the risk of trivializing important actions and making mundane what the philosophers have held high throughout history.

Indeed, writing under the *nom de plume* Peter Sacks, one college instructor recently described what life is like when his institution treated students as customers. "What the student-customer born and bred in such a [postmodern popular] culture wants is success; he wants it now, and he doesn't want to have to struggle to achieve it" (Sacks, 1996, p. 164). The author details his trials and tribulations with undergraduate teaching and argues that students want little more than easy grades, unchallenging assignments, and humorous professors. A customer-driven focus certainly runs the risk of destroying standards if the definition of such a focus is to blindly adapt to the marketplace and merely meet the whims of whoever comes to classes. In this light, academe is antithetical to a business and academe's clientele should not be customers.

But we ought not to get trapped in our language. Colleges and universities are engaged in intellectual transactions in much the same way that those in a church deal in spiritual transactions. In order to serve individuals, postsecondary organizations need improved customer focus. For too long, they have accepted the status quo and allowed their customers to discover that the courses they need in order to graduate are not offered in a timely fashion, that the coherence of the institution's course work is nonexistent, or that what someone thought their financial aid package was is actually different. What are the immediate implications of an organization that hopes to refocus its energies?

Emphasis on the Individual Over Rules

Students, alumni, parents, and other constituencies are dealt with in order to solve the issue at hand, rather than to explain why something cannot be done. College participants have been taught that if they explain *our* rules to *them,* then *they* will adapt. Sometimes, such explanations are important and necessary. A student who wants to take physics when he or she has not completed basic science is not being done a service when the adviser simply accedes to his or her demands. More often than not, however, individuals find explanations that do not try to meet the person's concerns, but rather convinces the student of the impracticality of them. An organization that wants to move toward reengineering communicates concern for the individual.

Emphasis on People's Needs Rather Than the Organization's Functions

"We offer an excellent education at an affordable price," tells individuals what the organization does. The overarching statement will inevitably drift downward to other segments of the organization so that one will find out that "student services has y function," or that the "school of education seeks to create educational leaders." Who can argue with an organization that desires excellence? The problem is that the people who create such statements appear to be working in a vacuum: "We organize so we can do these activities." Instead, what we need to hear is, "Our organization seeks to help people in specific ways." A college or university ought to emphasize people's needs first and then demonstrate how the institution's intellectual agendas respond to these needs, rather than casting a net about what the organization does and seeing if anyone is interested. A company or business or church highlights how it hopes to improve customers' lives. Colleges and universities need to communicate a similar concern.

Emphasis on New Members' Socialization

Colleges and universities are discipline-focused in their orientation for faculty, and function-focused for all other employees. When a department or school searches for a candidate, more often than not, they want the best English professor, or math professor, or biochemist. Search committees learn more about the candidates than they know about one another. Similarly, when a unit wants a new secretary or a business officer they seek people who can type or balance budgets. This is fine and good. Again, no one wants to argue against hiring individuals who are superb in a given field of expertise, be it Classics or word processing. However, an organization's participants need to communicate what their organization is about to new members. Organizations are distinct entities; the participants' inability to communicate what is important allows new members to fall back on external knowledge, rather than build on the knowledge they have coming into the organization and applying it in culturally specific ways for the organization.

Maintain Identity

In an organization that communicates an initial identity to new members, they most likely will find an ethic of care and concern. Socialization does not end after the first moments a new recruit enters the organization. Instead, socialization occurs through constant nurturing and concern on the part of those individuals who enact the new face of leadership I spoke about in Chapter 2. Participants in colleges and universities need something more than simply an organizational culture, since all organizations have cultures. A college or university that wants to reengineer begins by communicating how it honors the customer and how its work focuses on meeting that goal.

Emphasize the Uniqueness of the Organization

An organization that has a particular focus on customers will not be for everyone. An organization's participants need to understand that by stating who they are, and also by pointing out who they are not. Some individuals will decide that they do not want to work in such an organization, or more important, they will find that others are not a good fit for the kind of organization they desire. The light and dark of such a painting is that by clarifying who they are, they also obscure the belief that they can be something for everyone. Perhaps some good individuals will not want to work in such an organization. That's OK. People should work in organizations where they feel comfortable with the credo that is developed. As I noted earlier, the challenge for a college's participants at the close of the 20th century is to invoke meaning into their organizations. By such an invocation some will reject such meanings. The rejection is a positive sign because it points to self-definition, which is an essential first step in reengineering.

Thus, communication's chiaroscuro alternates between a clarifying light on what the organization is about, but also creates an understanding of what the organization is not about, and who will not fit. They highlight their focus on individuals and groups rather than functions and descriptions. They do not so much reject functions or descriptive commentary, but instead, comprehend that in order for meaning to develop around these activities, they first must communicate who they are, who they serve, and what they honor. Individuals who work in the organization are encouraged to make decisions rather than allow problems to become someone else's responsibility. Ownership is communicated throughout the organization.

Incentives

By and large, academic organizations traditionally have been flatter than other companies. The wage differential between the institution's president

TABLE 5.1 Median Salaries

Title	1969–1970	1985–1986	Increase 1970–1986	1995–1996	Increase 1986–1996	Increase 1970–1996
Presidents	25,979	65,899	154%	114,298	73%	440%
Assistant to President	15,167	40,711	168%	53,560	32%	353%
Director, Development	16,330	35,280	116%	75,000	113%	459%
Director, Financial Aid	10,409	29,639	185%	45,400	53%	436%
Professor	25,740	47,280	84%	73,610	56%	286%
Associate Professor	17,990	34,040	89%	51,920	53%	289%
Assistant Professor	14,550	28,460	96%	43,680	53%	300%
Instructor	11,460	20,990	83%	31,060	48%	271%

SOURCES: Data compiled from *Chronicle of Higher Education*, (1970, September 28), p. 12; *Chronicle* (1971, April 19), p. 4; *Chronicle* (1986, March 19), p. 24; *Chronicle* (1986, April 9), p. 25; *Chronicle* (1986, April 23), p. 25; *Chronicle* (1996, September 2), pp. 23-24.

and the lowest-paid assistant professor, although large, pales in comparison to that between the CEO and the new white-collar worker in a *Fortune 500* company. No one should attribute any terrific sense of democracy or socialism on the part of academe's participants here, but instead recognize how the market dictates compensation. Colleges and universities simply do not have the income available to pay their leaders millions of dollars a year.

Over the last generation salary differentials have risen dramatically (see Table 5.1). In 1969 an average president's salary was almost $26,000, and an assistant professor made slightly over $14,000. Today, we find that presidents earn over $114,000, and assistant professors earn less than $44,000.

We have seen almost a 500% increase in the salary of college presidents, but only a 300% increase for assistant professors. The result is that, while a generation ago, an assistant professor made 56% of what a president made, today the assistant professor earns only 38% of the average college president earns (see Tables 5.2 and 5.3).

To compound the problem, consider the retirement and benefits packages of chancellors and presidents. Such packages have only improved

TABLE 5.2 Differential Percentage Changes of Faculty Compared to Staff

	1969–1970	1985–1986	1995–1996	% of Decrease 1970–1996
Professor/President	99%	72%	64%	35%
Assistant Professor/ President	56%	43%	38%	18%
Associate Professor/ Director, Development	110%	96%	69%	41%
Assistant Professor/ Assistant to President	96%	70%	82%	14%
Instructor/Director, Financial Aid	110%	71%	68%	42%

NOTE: In 1970, an assistant professor made 56% of what a president made; by 1996, the assistant professor made only 38% of what a president made, a decrease of 18%. In 1970, a professor made 99% of what a president made; by 1996, the professor made 64% of what a president made, a decrease of 35%.

TABLE 5.3 Differential Percentage Changes of Administration Compared to Faculty

	1969–1970	1985–1986	1995–1996	% of Increase 1970–1996
President/Professor	101%	139%	155%	54%
President/ Assistant Professor	179%	232%	262%	83%
Director, Development/ Associate Professor	91%	104%	144%	53%
Assistant to President/ Assistant Professor	104%	143%	123%	72%
Director, Financial Aid/ Instructor	91%	141%	146%	54%

NOTE: In 1969 to 1970, a president of an institution made $25,979, while an assistant professor made $14,550, or 79% of the president's salary. In 1995 to 1996, a president made $114,298, while an assistant professor made $43,680, or 30% of the president's salary.

over time so that the actual salary and benefits of a college president today are vastly improved over those of the assistant professor who enters the academy.

One may very well quarrel with the admittedly imperfect numbers. Not all presidents earn such salaries. Some full professors (especially in the medical profession) earn salaries equivalent to, or greater than, their institution's president. Exceptions to rules always exist. Nevertheless, the basic trend is quite apparent: Over the last generation salary differentials between senior administrators and the faculty have increased significantly. The implications are twofold. Symbolically, a democratic culture takes a beating when economic or structural stratification increases rather than decreases. On a practical level one finds that fiscal incentives for chief executive officers have increased at a much greater rate than those for the faculty. Both implications are worrisome, and create problems for participants in an organization that desires to reengineer.

Academic organizations always have been a bit schizophrenic. Those who work in them like to think of themselves as a community of scholars, which implies that some kind of democracy exists. A community survives by the consent of the governed. The same would not be said for most businesses. The assumption is that academics have much greater control over the conditions of their work than most employees in standard for-profit businesses.

However, colleges and universities also exist by hierarchical rankings; full professors have more influence than associates, who have more influence than assistants, who have more influence than part-timers or instructors, who have none. Postsecondary organizations have collegial governance structures under which faculty ostensibly decide about academic issues. At the same time, there are boards of trustees that quite frequently hold significant amounts of influence over internal affairs of the institution and make decisions that are the opposite of what the faculty desire.

Previous research points out that strong, consistent cultures are more likely to be ready for creating change than those that are inconsistent and contradictory. When the symbols and actions of the organizations are consistent with the mission and purpose that is being espoused, there is greater likelihood that the organization's participants will be able to interpret matters in a consistent way. Conversely, contradictory messages stymie clear signals about what faculty and administrators intend or desire for the organization. I do not mean that everyone must march to the same academic drummer; however, one need not be a management expert to realize that an organization's participants are less likely to buy into risk taking or belt tightening when they discover that the president has redecorated the office and the trustees have taken a lavish retreat at the expense of the institution.

Symbols are often the only incentives change agents have to stimulate change. At many institutions today, salary raises of a few hundred dollars every other year are the best that can be done. How does one stimulate change in such an environment? One way is to applaud action in word and deed for those people who buy into reengineering. As I mentioned in the previous chapter, if individuals are to stimulate progress on a structural level, then they must ensure that the reward structure is in step with the goals. To say that the organization wants faculty to concentrate on their teaching, but then reward their research, clearly sends mixed signals, and creates confusion, if not anger, in much the same way as having the president say, "We need to tighten our belts," in one breath while he gives himself a raise in the next breath.

Symbolic incentives operate in multiple ways. At the simplest level, those words of encouragement that individuals provide to their colleagues on a consistent basis reinforce behavior. Similarly, awards, plaques, and public ceremonies that celebrate one's colleagues for a particular act that they deem in line with the organization's goals and missions help develop a sense of what the organization honors. Finally, when institutional participants incorporate in their own behavior the kind of work they desire from others they offer potent incentives for what they want.

Everyone has heard false or insincere words of encouragement. Everyone has attended public ceremonies that are painfully dull because they have the air of phoniness about them. The fact that an individual acts one way does not mean that everyone else will follow his or her lead. However, symbolic incentives are not meant to be management gimmicks or tools that are unhinged for broader cultural traditions and mores. If individuals are unable to internalize what the broad mission and fabric of the culture are, then they will be unable to develop and provide meaningful symbols that inspire and invigorate people to act.

Individuals learn from an incentive system that sets the stage for organizational expectations. Summative action is one way to engage reformers; individuals look at the cumulative work that someone has done and reward them for positive contributions. An additional way to create change is by influencing the process at the outset, rather than at the end. If individuals want to create change, then they need to set the stage. To a certain extent department chairs, but even more so deans and provosts, need to consider ways to encourage faculty to undertake activities that will help move the campus in a way that supports the organization's goals. I have often been surprised at how infrequently administrators use such incentives to stimulate change. Words and actions need to have some sort of symbiosis.

I mentioned above how redecorating one's office during a time of fiscal exigency sends a mixed signal. Similarly, if individuals talk about the importance of a particular undertaking but put no resources behind it, they also send a signal. When strategic plans seem to come and go at the whim of every new administrator who sets foot on campus, an organization's participants have good reason to wonder if what has been suggested as an "imperative" is yet another management fad.

If a campus, for example, desires to cut across schools or colleges and create interdisciplinary curricula, or wants an increased emphasis on distance learning, then they need to create the environment to make it possible. I mentioned earlier how individuals need to marshal their structures in such a way that enable cross-campus communication to occur. By all means, they also need to utilize the symbolic resources at their command, and they should recognize that people resonate to fiscal and intellectual incentives. Course buyouts, modest stipends in the summer, and assistance in the form of secretarial or student support and the like, are significant ways to stimulate interest and symbolize the import of the proposed changes. If the changes are unimportant, then no resources will be afforded them. If individuals take them seriously, they will provide incentives to stimulate reform.

The chiaroscuro of reform is a blend of symbolic and fiscal incentives. A particular symbolic act can be interpreted as hypocritical and false in one culture, while the exact same action will be essential in another. A fiscal incentive is "real" in one sense, but symbolic in another. We seek incentives that stimulate change on the one hand, but the incentives need to be culturally consistent. Radical reform within cultures is possible, but such change does not mean culture's dissolution. If anything, change is the clarification of meaning within a culture and the orchestrated and consistent interpretation of a multitude of symbols and incentives. Thus, *symbolic and fiscal incentives stimulate change by emphasizing core values and reaffirming organizational direction.*

Power and Control

Carol Axtell Ray (1986) has posited that culture is the last frontier of control, merely an updated version of bureaucracy. She certainly has a point. In a cynical or manipulative view of organizational life, managers try to concoct schemes to increase production from workers at their psychic and fiscal expense. "The latest strategy of control," observes Ray, "implies that the top management team aims to have individuals possess direct ties to the values and goals of the dominant elites in order to activate the emotion and sentiment which might lead to devotion, loyalty, and commitment to the company" (Ray, 1986, p. 294). Such a strategy "contains possibilities of being extremely powerful in ensnaring workers in a hegemonic system" (Ray, 1986, p. 295). In this light, virtually everything I have suggested with regard to the creation and maintenance of an organization's mission, strategy, and goals is little more than a ploy to manipulate the environment and people in order to have them fulfill the demands of management. Individuals are neither spiritually fulfilled in their work-lives, nor necessarily fiscally compensated in an equitable manner.

An organization's participants are mistaken if they overlook that aspect of culture and reengineering that will homogenize individuals rather than enable them to reach their fullest capacity. The development of binding ideologies and organizations with strong socializing tendencies does run the risk of manipulating, rather than enabling, people. Collins and Porras (1994) also have noted, albeit without the quasi-Marxist language, that visionary companies may act like cults, in that they run the risk of indoctrinating, rather than liberating, individuals.

The creative expression of an individual's will is essential if those in academe want to turn their colleges and universities into learning organizations where students are central and learning is key. Colleges and universities cannot afford automatons of mind or spirit en route to increasing productivity in a postmodern universe. Thus, individuals need to consider ways not to eliminate power or control in an organization, but rather to consider how to work with these concepts to ensure that the organizational climate enhances individual creativity and develops group ownership in the process. Such issues are of particular import as the organization begins to reengineer, for if the populace sees reengineering as yet another tool to manipulate them, they will not be able to implement change. Four initiatives exist that pertain to working with power and control within a culture.

Constructing Criticism

An organization that seeks to develop creativity and enable people to make their own decisions also has to be one which enables individuals to criticize one another regardless of their position within the organization. Top-down approaches to management will not countenance insubordination; workers risk fines or expulsion if they criticize the boss. In an organization that honors differences of opinion, individuals seek to create venues where open and helpful criticism is fostered and valued. The point here should not be misconstrued. I do not seek to turn organizational life either into daily psychodramas where the participants confront one another on an endless basis, or into reeducation camps where individuals are expected to confess their sins.

Helpful criticism within organizational life is unlike that which develops in psychotherapy or a family. Organizations are not families. The president is not the father or mother, because if this is the analogy, then the faculty are the children. One cannot decentralize decision making about important issues to children. The organization needs equals.

The sole purpose is not personal fulfillment or liberation. Rather, criticism within an organization is a means to an end. Change agents desire individuals to have the ability to criticize one another and their bosses in order to improve productivity, foment reengineering, and improve the quality of life of all the members of the campus community. An organization in which individuals do not feel free to criticize is one that is not ready for reengineering.

Harmful criticism is certainly not well advised. If criticism is handled ineptly or in a way different from what was intended, individuals may well experience unhelpful, and indeed destructive, consequences. As any teacher knows, there is an art to criticism. The point is not to blast someone into oblivion so that the student is intellectually crippled, emotionally devastated, or not able to continue. Instead, individuals strive to create a climate in which their criticism is seen as valued, trusted advice that encourages an individual to do a better job. Such a climate demands respect and the ability of the individual who proffers the criticism to do so in a way that is supportive and sincere. Also, there needs to be the willingness of the person who receives the critique to take it in the spirit in which it was intended, and a structure that enables all of these ingredients to blend.

For such an undertaking to be successful, individuals need to be socialized to the values of the organization and to realize that honest criticism is one of those values. One learns how to take and receive criticism over time and in structured settings. Again, I am not suggesting that an organization's participants involve themselves in marathon critiques of one another, but having semiannual reviews where individuals are able to speak openly is one step in the right direction. Training of department chairs, deans, and other supervisory staff not simply about how to receive criticism, but also about how to create the ability to be criticized is helpful.

Reviewing Administration

In a previous chapter, I discussed the importance of performance reviews for faculty as communal discussions about the nature of their work. In an organization that seeks to reengineer, one's colleagues need to have a clear understanding about what the individual hopes to accomplish, how they might help the individual accomplish goals, and what the person might need to do to reorient his or her work to come into line with the mission of the institution. Such dialogues can often be intimidating and difficult.

If administrators are to be leaders, and if leadership in some small way pertains not only to what one says but more importantly to what one does, then one way to foment dialogue and carry the earlier point about constructive engagement further is for administrators to clarify how they are to be reviewed and ensure that such review occurs formally, professionally, and with multiple groups. All too frequently, a president reviews a provost who reviews the deans who review the department chairs who review the faculty. This chain of command approach to evaluation is top-down in nature and makes quite clear who has power and control and who does not. Why would a dean listen to his faculty, or a provost to her deans if the person responsible for her or his evaluation is the immediate superior? Rather than dialogical and consultative, management becomes a way to placate, intimidate, or simply control.

Certainly, the risk exists of witch hunts or badly managed review processes. It is also possible to envision pro forma reviews where someone might be able to say that multiple constituencies were consulted in a process, but the statement is more fiction than fact. Any undertaking is open to manipulation if individuals do not want to take it seriously or desire to subvert it. I am suggesting a more straightforward approach that in effect moves the organization away from military-style chains of command and toward processes where individuals learn that evaluation is a group task that involves all individuals, not only those who are powerful. What more apt signal exists that power is to be shared than when individuals develop an honest, fair process for subordinates to review and assess the work of those individuals above them?

Enabling Mistakes

If the organization's participants are going to take risks, then sometimes individuals are going to fail. How the group handles failure may be as important as how they handle success. There are a multitude of levels and kinds of mistakes. I am not speaking of unethical behavior or a consistent level of unsatisfactory work. Instead, I am thinking of honest efforts at improving the organization that have been well thought out and discussed, but that nevertheless involve an element of risk-taking. Reengineering, by definition, involves risk. If individuals learn that they will be sanctioned or penalized if they try something different from the norm, then they are not going to experiment. Conversely, if creativity is encouraged and individuals see others who have tried a new idea but for one reason or another it did not succeed, then the culture supports change rather than the status quo.

Cultural Audits

Any organization needs self-assessments to gauge progress and goal completion. In an organization that is about to reengineer, a cultural audit is equally important. I often reject the idea that outside consultants are necessary to bring about effective change. But frequently, before an organization begins a process of structural and cultural change, an outsider's views about the organization can provide a clear idea of who has power, who has control. I raise this issue because individuals often deceive themselves about themselves or their organization. A college president, for example, believes she has an open-door policy, but no one else in the organization feels that he or she could even walk through the door without an appointment (Tierney, 1988). A different college president reads the mission of the institution in one way, but significant constituencies such as students and townspeople read it differently (Chaffee & Tierney, 1988). Faculty interpret the curriculum one way, students another (Tierney, 1989).

A cultural audit is akin to a health checkup or an accreditation visit, but rather than taking an individual's pulse or reading budget figures, the cultural auditor tries to come to terms with underlying themes of power and control. Often, an organization's participants will confide to an outsider what an insider is either unwilling or unable to hear. The purpose of an audit is not so much to prescribe solutions, but rather to offer a mirror for the organization to see a composite of itself as others see it. With such information the organization's participants will have an additional task, first to define where they agree or disagree with the assessment and then to discuss and debate possible routes of action. The underlying goal is to come to terms with how power and control function not merely by the lines of authority, but informally as well. Once individuals understand how people perceive one another and their organization, they will be better prepared to move particular aspects of the organization to create change.

Here chiaroscuro works in linguistic contrasts. Individuals recognize that power cannot be eliminated, but they nonetheless try to make sense of it. They acknowledge that organizational structures and lines of authority surely exist, but they seek to interpret them and look behind them for invisible structures of power and control. They assume that any process has potential for failure, but they nonetheless accept that if reform is to occur they must come to terms with the cultural processes in which change is embedded. Individuals must *struggle to understand and alter traditional notions of power and control by using cultural tools.*

Information

Perhaps no part of managerial life has changed more dramatically in the last decade than has information; who gets it, what individuals get, and most importantly, how it is disseminated. I have visited some institutions where internal correspondence by paper is something of the past and everyone uses e-mail. At another institution the faculty handbook is on the web and only a handful of individuals still own a paper copy. For my own part, I receive about 50 e-mail messages a day, from colleagues a few doors down the hall and others who are overseas.

The temptation is to say that such transformations in technology have vastly improved the organization's information systems. In periods of rapid upheaval, however, rather than improve systems, individuals might first acknowledge that they have simply changed. In some respects the process has been democratized insofar as more people have the potential for access to more information. Procedures also have accelerated so that information that might have taken weeks to get now can be delivered in a matter of minutes. Dialogues with diverse individuals and groups that may well not have occurred without these technologies is also possible. For those who believe that informality is positive, e-mail also has cultivated a casual style far different from letters and memos.

Yet no one should assume that any tool is a panacea. Humans still drive the response system. Humanity's foibles, assumptions, and beliefs help create what the system is becoming. And we are not sure what the system should become. By now most e-mail users have probably been on the receiving end of a "flame," when someone writes or responds in an uncharacteristically angry manner. That anger would most likely have been hidden or at least toned down if the parties involved were speaking face-to-face, or even over the phone. Similarly, if individuals assume that the same people should receive the same information as before, only in an electronic version, then little has changed with regard to decision making and strategy. Conversely, if an organization's participants believe that everyone should receive voluminous amounts of information on any and every topic, then the organization's participants are overwhelmed with the mistaken belief that more is better. One consequence is that individuals may misconstrue a piece of information, interpret it in a manner that was not intended, and create an immediate uproar over the Internet that may not have occurred in a pre-electronic-mail era.

The information system has then changed. The ultimate effect of electronic technologies on college and university life is still to be seen, but my assumption is that the changes are going to be much more far-reaching than simply moving from standard to electric typewriters. However, the changes may not all improve the organization. As with other innovations I have outlined here, organizations need leadership and management of the process. Otherwise, change will come willy-nilly without forethought about how such changes affect the entire organization. Such changes, however, afford individuals a dual opportunity to consider (1) how to employ new tools in implementing reform, and (2) how such tools might help an organization's participants rethink current managerial structures. In short, how might technological changes enable a college or university to redesign organizational processes so that a student and learning-centered institution emerges?

Information and the Implementation of Reform

All too frequently information becomes an end in itself. The organization consumes faculty and administrative time with completing surveys and forms in different formats for diverse constituencies. The amount of time it takes to complete forms and then compile them creates the sense that reporting, rather than reform, is what concerns individuals. Obviously, in an organization concerned with reengineering, people desire change, not simply facts and figures that get prepared for one office or another.

It is also a mistake to assume that the lack of resources, such as computers, web sites, or the latest experiments in audiovisual aids is what stymies change. Such tools help stimulate reform, but they are means to ends, not ends in themselves. Technology and information aid individuals in the movement to where they are going, but do not provide the road map. Without a map and compass that provide the organization with direction, technologies mindlessly speed up processes that are in need of fundamental reform. As Hammer and Champy (1993) note, "Reengineering, unlike automation, is about innovation. It is about exploiting the latest capabilities of technology to achieve entirely new goals. One of the hardest parts of reengineering lies in recognizing the new, unfamiliar capabilities of technology instead of its familiar ones" (p. 85). The technology revolution is not only about making individuals do the same tasks more efficiently, but in enabling individuals to do different tasks so that they are more productive, effective, and ultimately, efficient. Efficiency, in and of itself, is not an end.

Thus, the organization's actors have two simultaneous tasks. One is to orient themselves to how the organization might use new processes to reconfigure what they want to do, and the other is to provide incentives and training to individuals to use the new technologies. In doing so, the goal is not to replace what they have been doing, but to stimulate thinking about alternative ways of doing what they have been doing. The following are ways one might use information and technology in vastly different manners.

Admissions

Colleges and universities often admit students in a serial manner. One committee puts the file together, another reviews it, then another, and finally it goes to a series of administrators. Applications could be reviewed simultaneously so that an institution dramatically speeds up the process, aids the consumer, and cuts down on paperwork and staff time.

Advising

Faculty and administrators have long wrung their hands about the woeful state of advising and counseling. Some argue faculty are inept at counseling and the organization needs to train them; others say yet another office for advising should be created. Personal and socio-psychological services is certainly a significant issue that needs to be addressed. But the vast majority of students or applicants simply want correct answers to their queries about their courses of study. "When will course x be offered; do I have to take y; they just cut off my financial aid, what do I do?" The norm is that postsecondary institutions bounce students around from office to office and often give conflicting advice. An integrated system can solve this problem so that virtually all employees respond immediately and correctly to students' questions.

Meetings

Perhaps the greatest complaint of university personnel of all stripes is the amount of time one wastes in committee meetings. If the organization adequately trains people how to develop constructive dialogues in cyber-space, personal time can be enhanced, and the need for constant meetings will be lessened.

Decisions

Researchers frequently have argued that managers decide because they have the information. In an electronic age it is possible to decentralize decisions if the organization's participants enable those closest to the task to have information that previously may have been held by only a few senior level administrators.

Interactions

One point that continues to amaze me is the degree to which consumer tastes change. Individuals have long felt, for example, that students desire one-on-one interaction with faculty and staff. Again, to a certain degree this point still holds true. But it is also certain that many students are more adept and comfortable with new technologies than the faculty or staff. Students often would prefer to interact over the "net" and have their questions and concerns answered immediately rather than have to wait a week for an appointment to see an instructor, an associate dean, or a student services counselor. A faculty member frequently prefers an answer to a question from the department chair or dean rather than having to play telephone tag.

Faculty, staff, and administrators utilize existing technologies to con-sider ways to change. They educate their personnel on how to capitalize on technology to undertake work in new patterns. They anticipate changes by constantly striving to consider where they are going rather than where they are.

Rethinking Structure

Where have individuals traditionally held, developed, and disseminated information, and where have they not? In general, data gathering has been done in one of two ways. On the one hand, collecting information has been sporadic at best, and there has been no clearinghouse or agent for accumulating and analyzing data. On the other, institutions have an office of institutional research traditionally lodged close to a president's office. They collect data that the president or provost deems important. The first response is inadequate and the second needs to be reconfigured if individuals want to prepare to reengineer.

The lack of adequate information over time enables everyone to draw upon whatever criteria they desire in defining where the organization or unit should go. There is not one best decision or finite, perfect criterion upon which to base organizational decisions. Indeed, a primary focus of a reengineered organization is to determine which criteria among the multitude that are available to an organization will be used in decision-making. Thus, the need exists for consistent databases that enable all constituencies to develop clear criteria for measuring organizational excellence. I am suggesting neither that one informational system and database fits all organizational units, nor that individuals should mindlessly fill in forms to prove that everyone is performing in a manner consistent with everyone else. Still, without some sense that an organization has data to share with one another, individuals have no ability to marshal and evaluate collective activities geared toward a common vision such as making the organization student and learning centered. Goals have to be judged. Far too often evaluative efforts are simply matters of reporting rather than analyzing how a unit did.

In an educational organization everyone needs to think of themselves as educators in one form or another. Offices of institutional research, combined with schools or departments of education, and libraries have a critical role to play with regard to reengineering. As Judith Stiehm (1994) writes,

> Universities have as their unique charge education. One might expect that their central school, their keystone, the domain of their most honored scholars would be a school of education. One might also expect universities to study themselves, to collect data to help them enhance their teaching and scholarship. The truth is that schools of education are low in most institutional hierarchies and the offices of institutional research tend to address managerial issues rather than educational concerns. (p. 152)

Without going into an exegesis about why schools of education have low status, allow me to agree with Stiehm and slightly reformat her comment in order to adapt it to reengineering. Those who work in colleges and universities ought never forget that their central purpose for being in existence is geared toward education, broadly defined. Indeed, given the sea change that is occurring in society at large, those in postsecondary institutions are likely to have even broader conceptions of education to consider in the future, rather than fewer. Educational issues must always be at the forefront of what faculty, staff, and administrators do and how they gauge their progress. Offices of institutional research need to be at the interstices of educational life, rather than at its bureaucratic fringes. Schools of education, in a similar vein, ought to help build dialogue about educational technologies and new ideas about teaching and learning excellence for the academic community. Libraries also have the potential to advance learning in ways that exist within and beyond the classroom. Each of these units might be reconceptualized in part to have more to do with the other, rather than operating totally independently and in isolation from them.

Previously, the norm has been to think of units as discrete entities that vie for resources and carry out activities quite separate from one another. However, in an age where technology is exploding and culturally developed information systems are mandatory, organizational participants need to think of ways to enhance dialogues about their purposes and how they evaluate them. In doing so, offices ought not be repositories of data for external authorities, or staffed by lonely managers whom the rest of the organization's participants neither know, nor feel they need to know. These three units in part form the service component of both soft projects and the standing structure. Schools of education still will train teachers, libraries still will hold books in ways they have done for centuries, and IR offices still will send reports to external authorities who demand particular documents. Nevertheless, *information technology creates the conditions for reengineering by helping individuals think about not what exists, but what might exist.*

Herein lies the portrait done in chiaroscuro. Where an organization once had clear lines of who received information and what the information was, the lines are now less clear. Individuals now see shades in different arenas that are blurred. Eyes gaze not on the specific moment in which the organization exists, but on the unclear outlines of future possibilities. Those who are the organization's Rembrandts, their chiaroscurists, are people in reconceptualized offices of institutional research, schools of education, and libraries.

Against Strategy

There are certain terms individuals use when discussing organizational life that often have no logical opposites. Who can be against "streamlining" a decision-making process or implementing a plan that involves "continuous quality"? Also, who does not want institutional leaders to be strategic in their thinking? In *Academic Strategy*, George Keller (1983) wrote:

> To have a strategy is to put your own intelligence, foresight, and will in charge instead of outside forces and disordered concerns. The priorities are always there. The question is who selects them. . . . Strategy means agreeing on some aims and having a plan to defeat one's enemies, or to arrive at a destination, through the effective use of resources. (p. 75)

At first blush, one might assume that strategy is precisely what the organization needs. Indeed, I have written in an earlier chapter about how plans put into action the goals and visions of the college or university. No one wants "outside forces" or "disordered concerns" driving organizational life. And individuals most certainly do not want to succumb to their enemies or use resources ineffectively.

Nevertheless, it is important to recognize what I have emphasized throughout the book: Words and action are interpretive and the manner in which an organization's actors interpret them have implications for the organization. If individuals use Keller's commonly accepted definition of academic strategy then they should be against it for the organization that seeks to reengineer. Just as individuals ought to be against efficiency if the idea is tied to nothing other than blindly cutting costs, one cannot subscribe to strategic thinking if it is little more than developing an enemies' list and defeating them with a battle plan developed by the outmoded metaphor of generals leading their troops.

Indeed, anyone who employs strategy in this manner works against organizational redesign. "Have you learned nothing?" one might ask the college president who thinks of herself or himself as a field commander rallying the troops. If the "priorities are always there," as Keller's statement implies, individuals wrongly assume that reality's choices await them; regardless of who is in charge, if he or she understands strategic thinking well enough, then the right option will be chosen. Thus, the individual who seeks to reengineer his or her postsecondary institution and sets in motion a strategic planning process, whereby a leader alerts the troops to the problems and solutions, is actually changing the structure and culture of the traditional organization in minimal ways. The old idea of strategic planning, then, is little more than trying to bring order to a disorderly process. When all is said and done, little has changed.

No less an authority than Henry Mintzberg, one of the founding fathers of strategy, has written, "Strategy can blind the organization to its own datedness. . . . Strategies are to organizations what blinders are to horses; they keep them going in a straight line, but impede the use of peripheral vision" (Mintzberg, 1987b, p. 32). In this light, strategic planning's strength is also its weakness, especially in times when organizations need to change. Strategic planning is a tool for organizations to use in maintaining order and setting direction during stable times. Individuals concentrate on doing the little tasks that consume organizational life rather than constantly change direction.

But have I not argued in a previous chapter that organizations suffer from attention deficit disorder and that they need to be consistent, be strategic? Well, yes and no.

Herein lies the chiaroscuro of strategy. An organization's participants have a clarity, a lightness, about the core of the organization, but it is less clear with regard to other points. Individuals develop, foment, a creativity and innovativeness that enables them to work without blinders.

Collins and Porras (1994) point out that one myth of organizational life is that those businesses that have been most successful are the ones that developed complex, even brilliant, strategic plans. To the contrary, "visionary companies," write Collins and Porras, "make some of their best moves by experimentation, trial and error, opportunism, and—quite literally, accident" (1994, p. 9). How, then, do an organization's participants deal with the seeming schizophrenia of my suggesting in one chapter that they do not pay enough attention to what they are doing, and in the next that they should not obsess about what they do?

The leader who comes out against strategic planning should anticipate an outcry. "A rudderless ship," "working blind," "blowing in the wind," "just responding to the whims of the marketplace," are phrases likely to be heard. Perhaps, then, the leader should not speak against strategy, but seek a third way. Rather than be for or against strategy, conceive of strategy within the framework of reengineering. Do not focus on continuing to "do the right thing," but to invent "new things." In this light, *strategy functions beyond the boxes; it stimulates learning and a passion to undertake new activities by multiple actors.*

"Planning's failure," observes Mintzberg, "to transcend the categories explains why it has discouraged serious organizational change" (Mintzberg, 1994, p. 109). The norm of a new college president is that she or he will set in motion a series of orchestrated dialogues that results in a detailed strategic plan where one of two results occurs: Either it is dead on arrival and goes unused, or it is employed as a prescription for an illness that is continued to be used whether it cures or kills the patient. What's a leader to do? How do we begin reform efforts?

The Double Core

College and university participants are often pressed into action by multiple needs, forces, and constituencies. Quite frequently, internal political processes drive decisions. One task that cannot be done too frequently is to ask three questions at the conclusion of a meeting:

1. Are the institution and its employees better off because of what we have decided?
2. Are students better served by the decisions we have just made?
3. Have we enhanced the environment for teaching, learning, and research by what we have just done?

The organization's actors need to realize what they do when they raise such questions. They move the group away from the focus on individualism and toward communal goals. If the individual is a good politician and he or she is able to reduce his or her teaching load from x courses a year to x-1, the professor may well be able to claim that the decision has improved life, but the institution may suffer either because students have fewer opportunities to take courses, or fewer options, or the costs of the school rise. That should not be the objective. The group must continually strive in the creation of plans to focus on these core questions.

At times, answers to such questions may be indirect. The decision to change the institution's logo usually has little to do with whether the teaching and learning environment improves. However, an organization should be able to point out how what they have done has worked for organizational improvement. And as importantly, it brings to the forefront of organizational focus, the *raison d'être*. If individuals cannot respond in any meaningful way to the questions, then they rightfully might question their decisions. To be sure, they can fool themselves or answer such questions monochromatically. If that is the intent, then do not waste time asking the questions. Those who are interested in dramatic change, however, raise questions in order for the group to ponder the answers, rather than simply as rhetorical devices for management.

If those are generic questions that any institution might ask of itself, then the second core is specific to the culture of the organization in which individuals work. These are the kinds of questions college or university participants ask in the development, maintenance, and reconfiguration of basic mission statements. Strategies, properly devised, stimulate change while maintaining core values; if the core is healthy and in sync with the enacted environments that surround them. Obviously, a core value that focuses on self-centeredness or remuneration only for those who complain the most is not a healthy core. A core that maintains a specific religious identity when the feeder schools have closed and the surrounding community has changed is not necessarily viable any longer.

Thus, a strategy is more like a gestalt than a battle plan. It enhances reflective thought about who *we* are and if the organization is performing in ways that support one another. Strategies are ideas, or as Mintzberg (1987a) has observed, "dreams in search of a reality" (p. 17). The role of change agents is to help create the reality.

Dualistic Thinking

At the same time, an organization's participants constantly have to fight the temptation to obsess about who they are. It is critical to hold two contradictory ideas at the same time. Individuals focus on the double core, but they do not rethink at every turn what they do, or undo what has been done. There is something to be said for making a decision and moving on. Faculties are infamous for the opposite. They analyze an issue from every conceivable angle, study the topic a bit more, finally make a decision at the last meeting of the school year, only to discover that a new committee the next year has decided to rethink what they have done. This form of stop and go is not what I am suggesting; such a model exemplifies shared gridlock, not shared governance.

Rather, think of those constants in one's life that cause reflection. Individuals do not arise every morning and wonder if they should remain in their relationship with their partner or spouse. They generally do not go to sleep every night wondering if it is time to leave their job. If their personal and work relationships are healthy, loving, and productive, more often than not they monitor what goes on in them and constantly tinker at improving them. If they do not care for and nurture them, they will suffer. And, at times, individuals get a divorce or leave their jobs or suffer a trauma that undeniably changes their relationships.

We ought to approach strategy in similar fashion. A strategy is not a book on a shelf that one merely nods at as he or she goes about everyday business. Instead, strategies are with individuals in their decision making and planning. They use them as reference points for thinking about what they want to do, and as springboards for action. Although they are not set in stone, they also are not an Etch-a-Sketch® that would go away at the shake of a wrist. They help individuals synthesize hard and soft data so that they are then able to plan concretely what to do.

Planning's Double

For years I have taught a doctoral seminar on qualitative methodology. One of the tasks students often stumble over is walking themselves through their research project. They may have a well-developed theoretical framework, have solved the "so what" problem that has plagued generations of graduate students, and actually have a workable research design; but they do not have a flight plan and are often stymied about how to develop one. It is as if they are airline pilots who have passed all their course work, know they want to fly from New York to Los Angeles, have the skills to fly the plane, and now want to get in the plane and take off. I have learned over time that walking one's self through a qualitative project from start to finish is a skill like any other, and the ability to do it is one marker of whether the individual will produce a good dissertation.

Qualitative research inevitably involves deviations from the plan. The researcher plans to interview a specific set of individuals and realize midway through the project that he also must interview another set, or that interesting data might be found in a site he could not have known about prior to the beginning of the project. Someone else begins with a good interview protocol and discovers that some of the questions are poorly phrased, or not understood in the manner she had intended, so she changes them. All such modifications are fine, I tell my students, as long as they remain clear about their purpose and where they want to be going. If they enter the field without a clear purpose or plan, they are likely to waste a good deal of time and energy trying to discover what they want to discover. All too frequently, they do not finish their work but throw up their hands in desperation.

The same point can be made about strategies and planning. Individuals ought not fool themselves that a plan is so specific that they have a cookbook. They also should not assume that they can take off without one. I frequently have been mystified on my travels when I consult with a dean or president who has a good idea about what he or she wants to do, but is unable to articulate how to get the institution from point A to point B. Individuals who begin without their plans often do not end up where they wish to go, but end up where they have been pushed. In an earlier chapter I discussed how projects need clear goals and objectives. What I am urging here is that prior to embarking on a project, an organization's participants consider the steps they need to take to achieve the goals.

Planning's double, then, is in keeping with the intent of this section's cultural view of strategic planning. On the one hand, individuals develop plans that stimulate progress while maintaining the core identity, but on the other hand they also do not want a rigid agenda. They remain clear about what they want to accomplish so that they do not get sidetracked onto other issues. Yet they also have an approach open to modification and alteration along the way. Individuals do not make up numbers about time or money or personnel, but they also do not begin without any real sense of what it will take to accomplish the project.

Strategies

I began this section with George Keller's maxim to defeat the enemy. In a reengineered organization individuals ought not waste their energy at overcoming a real or imagined enemy. They do not develop strategies like a field commander in order to overwhelm the enemy. A college or university that seeks to reengineer moves individuals away from venting symbolic capital on mythic opponents and toward internal drives to do better.

The strategic process in which individuals are engaged is one that asks, "How can we do better and have we improved learning by what we have just done?" rather than developing a plan to advance on the enemy. By organizational improvement, faculty and administrators may well capture a market, move up in rankings, or earn greater research dollars, but these are by-products of reform rather than the goals themselves. Strategies, like goals, are for internal consumption. They help individuals make sense of pompous visionary language. They ground actions to ensure that individuals refer back to common purposes as they engage in any number of paths toward organizational redesign and the enhancement of learning.

6

The 21st Century Organization

Nothing will ever be attempted if all possible objections must be first overcome.

—Samuel Johnson

I argued at the outset of this book that whether we like it or not, change is upon us. We have no choice; those who work in colleges and universities must fundamentally rethink how they undertake their work. Change for change's sake, though not necessarily bad, soaks up a great amount of effort if individuals do not have a clear idea of why they are undertaking change. In an organization, modest changes for one reason or another may have little effect on the overall climate or results of the company, but the kind of wholesale reform that I have discussed here would be foolhardy to attempt on a whim or for the sake of it.

Although academe may have no choice about the need for change, the kind of changes that might be implemented are quite varied. James Duderstadt (1997) has observed how critical it is to define the real challenges of transforming institutions. "The challenge is rarely financial," he writes, "or organizational. It more frequently is the degree of cultural change that is required. We're faced with the challenge of transforming a set of rigid habits and thoughts" (Duderstadt, 1997, p. 12). Such changes need guiding principles that frame how to proceed. Without such principles an organization's participants are rudderless, capable of moving in any direction or in no direction at all. Formless activity is a path to certain failure since different parts of the organization move in any way without clear demarcations of success or failure. Instead, an organization's participants need a sense of what is important in order to define where they are to go and how they are to get there. If academe is to be responsive to the challenges that exist, then colleges and universities need to develop ways of interacting and communicating with different constituencies in ways dramatically different from what has previously been done.

I outlined in the introduction the commitments an academic community ought to make as it undertakes reengineering:

- A commitment to an educational community
- A commitment to academic freedom
- A commitment to access and equity
- A commitment to excellence and integrity
- A commitment to inquiry

These points help frame where colleges and universities are to go, but they do not suggest what the redesigned organization will look like. In what follows, I offer three components of what those who work in a college or university setting might look for as they redesign their organization. The first section summarizes how these organizations will be different from the present. The second section considers the foci of organizational work in a redesigned organization. I conclude by reiterating the guiding points that will help to redesign the organization, rather than merely make tidy changes within it.

Tomorrow's College

Less attention to structure, more attention to culture. The 20th century has been a time of structure building during which colleges and universities have gone from relatively meager entities with few structures and chains of command to institutions that have administrators to manage administrators, and programs within departments within divisions within schools within colleges within universities. The pitched battles that occur and the political maneuvering that takes place frequently happen over structural turf. Someone proposes that a department should be closed; an administrator wants a larger portfolio; a service area lobbies for more resources for the staff.

The kind of changes I have suggested move away from such concerns. Surely, structure still exists, and individuals still try to gain a greater piece of the fiscal pie. Organizational redesign does not do away with human foibles and concerns; it only restructures them. And that is the point.

Our obsession with structure is replaced by a more overt concern with culture. The sharp rigidity that we currently find in academe gives way to more fluidity, more ability to focus on soft projects, and more potential for individuals to cross departmental boundaries as their work and needs change. Structure in the kind of postmodern environment in which individuals currently reside impedes experimentation and innovation.

As with its radical fiscal counterpart, programmatic budgeting, the fallout from structural rigidity is twofold. First, those within the particular unit work for the unit rather than the larger entity. Second, the impetus to work with one another across structural boundaries is lessened.

In a reengineered world the focus shifts. Discussions about culture in an organization often happen toward the end of any decision-making schema. Decision-makers usually move structures around, discuss personnel, and draw up a battle plan or "strategy," as I mentioned in Chapter 5 and, as they head out the door, they point out that they need to massage the culture to make this happen. Such commentary underscores the lack of concern individuals all too often have for an organization's culture. Culture is the stepchild of decision making; individuals work on it when they have time.

In a redesigned organizational world, individuals turn such thinking on its head. The maintenance and nurture of culture becomes one of the main tasks of all employees, especially those who are the reputed leaders of the organization. Technology has enabled some individuals to work from home or on the road; the need to sit at a desk from 9 to 5 will increasingly dissipate. Nevertheless, individuals will still work in an organization. They need to find meaning, and such meaning does not come singularly by way of the department or division in which someone works. Instead, it will come through the often microscopic activities that take place throughout a day that enable an individual to feel part of an entity. Through such activities, individuals come to understand the basic purposes and goals of the organization in which he or she is involved. Rather than a new president arriving at work and focusing on the organizational chart, reporting lines, and the strengths and weaknesses of the institution from a bureaucratic perspective, the individual involved in reengineering will ask himself or herself questions such as

- What is the culture here?
- What do people define as important, and how do they define it?
- How does the culture deal with change?

Less Administration, Greater Faculty Flexibility

The 20th-century organization was earmarked by two expansions with different emphases. Institutions moved from being a president and a handful of faculty who taught classes, to organizations with a myriad of services and faculty who engage in multiple activities. Past practices ought not be looked on as mistakes or with a sense of regret. College students in the post-World War II era needed and demanded different kinds of services from the mostly privileged students at the turn of the 20th century. Day care, evening courses, remedial education, athletic facilities, and counseling are but a few examples of the remarkable expansion of non-teaching services that are commonplace on many campuses. The result has been an exponential growth in administration.

Concomitantly, the size of faculty has grown. While administration has branched out into multiple roles and responsibilities, the largest increase in faculty in the 20th century has been in tenure line positions. As I noted earlier, the growth has slowed, but the battle lines about tenure often have obscured discussions about the multiple roles that faculty might assume that do not fit traditional tenure criteria.

The redesigned organization will experience changes, both by demand and by the scope that reengineering takes. Colleges and universities need less, not more, administration. On the one hand, the consumer will demand fewer services. More students will desire an education, stripped down, and have less interest or need in the potpourri of services that colleges and universities offer. Organizational redesign also calls for less "administration of administration" so that colleges and universities will have greater authority further down in the organization and less need to monitor people in a way that has become the norm in the late 20th century.

Tenure will remain as a bulwark of academic freedom; if anything, the protections surrounding academic freedom must expand. But, so too will we discover an expansion of faculty roles that are not tenure track; the individuals who fill those positions, full-time and part-time, will be valued members of the organization. Thus, professors will assume multiple roles rather than the current lockstep that colleges and universities have with regard to teaching, research, and service.

Perhaps no change presents itself as great a challenge and a threat as the reconfiguration of faculty roles. Reengineering will not occur if it is seen as yet another attempt to do away with tenure and intrude upon faculty rights. As Duderstadt (1997) comments, "true faculty participation in the design and implementation of any transformation effort is absolutely necessary since the transformation of the faculty culture is the greatest challenge that we face" (p. 12).

If the procedures of reengineering were simply a managerial tool to exercise greater administrative power, I would not advocate it as a way to guide change into the future. However, reengineering is a tool like any other that ultimately is used by humans with purposes and ideals. I have pointed out from the beginning that two of the commitments we must main- tain are to academic freedom and to inquiry. As individuals reconfigure the organization they will also discover ways to bolster their ideals.

- What are core administrative activities?
- Which activities are not?
- What types of faculty work currently exist?
- What kind of work needs to exist?
- How do an institution's participants provide protection for academic freedom if they hire faculty without tenure status?

Less Differentiation Across Sectors, Greater Segmentation of Tasks Within Sectors

We have experienced two ecological changes to postsecondary organizations; one continues the traditional evolutionary approach to academe; the other is a natural ecological process. Academe has long been thought of as a place to retreat, an "ivory tower," where scholars ponder great questions divorced from everyday life, concerns, and worries that exist in society. The portrait has certainly changed over time, but in general the borders of a campus are as sharp today as they were 100 years ago. Society has defined sectors, such as K-12, community colleges, colleges and

universities, businesses and industry, and these sectors have little coordination or dialogue with one another. Academe has relied on a model under
which one sector goes it alone and the assumption is that each sector will
be able to carve out a niche for itself.

We also have worked from a hierarchical model within the postsecondary system that is mainly a product of this century. Research universities are at the top and community colleges are at the bottom. In the eyes
of many, trade and technical schools are off the map; they do not even
warrant discussion. The result, logically enough, is that everyone wants
to move up. Community colleges want to become 4-year institutions.
Normal schools became state colleges, and then state universities. The
state universities want to become research institutions. Many individuals
would look at such changes as natural results of a population ecology
approach to the environment. Organizations, like organisms, evolve in
one way in order to adapt, survive, and thrive.

Reengineering and the needs of the 21st-century move postsecondary
organizations in an alternative direction. If individuals are able to break
down barriers within the organization, then they also must seek ways to
communicate and cooperate with colleagues in other sectors. As opposed
to a model of an organization as a disengaged entity that has little desire
to work with other organizations, the 21st-century college or university
seeks out relationships that will foster innovation, change, and cross-
sector projects. Simply stated, an organization's participants cannot expect
their own organizations to undergo dramatic change if they do not
reconfigure how they operate with other organizations. To say that faculty
are able to work beyond the traditional trinity of research, teaching, and
service, but not to engage in dialogues with community or business-related
organizations about what they need, is to move in one direction without
taking the necessary action in a parallel arena. Similarly, to say that
administration should shrink and that postsecondary institutions will do
less of certain activities suggests that other units within society either will
assume those roles, or they will decide not to perform them.

What society expects of different institutional types needs to be
reconfigured. Organizational redesign does not mean that every organization is doing the same activities. Some segments of the postsecondary
universe will need to concentrate more fully on graduate education, while
others will focus on workplace education. The drift toward one model
whereby faculty are expected to do one task seems foolhardy at a time
when society needs greater differentiation, not less, and we are using a

research tool, reengineering, that calls for nurturing an individual organizational identity rather than assuming that abstract management process can turn out similar goals. What are three potential organizations with which the organization might become involved in strategic engagement? What differentiates the institution from others?

Circular Foci

Focus on results by focusing on processes. "We are obsessed with results," writes James Belasco (1990). "The process of achieving those results often is less important" (Belasco, 1990, p. 238). Whether it be America's long-standing concern to beat the rest of the world on test scores in grade school math, worries about affirmative action because the person with the highest SAT score may not win a spot in college, or businesses' attention to the "bottom line," Americans want to win. It may appear that I, too, have bought into the process. Recall an earlier chapter where I pointed out that results matter. Simply because someone is constantly writing an article, or because people are trying hard, does not mean we are fulfilling our potential or making progress. For too long academe has been goal free.

However, attention to organizational redesign calls for constant attention to process. An admissions officer will not succeed if he or she is simply concerned with numbers on a page that record more or fewer students than the previous year. Teachers ought not feel confident of success if the grade sheet records all "A's" and they have no sense of the processes taken to achieve those grades. Instead, the underlying assumption of reengineering is that the constant focus on process will reshape how to achieve what an organization's participants achieve, and in doing so, goals will be reached. Attention to process helps the organization's participants meet their goals.

By attention to process we bring into consideration how to treat students, external clients, and one another. We enhance culture. It is important to note that presidents and department chairs are neither psychotherapists nor gurus. However, an organization's participants do need to realize that colleges and universities are different places today than they were a generation ago, and that the simple manipulation of structure will no longer produce the desired results. Instead, change agents must constantly reevaluate how to attempt what the organization does, and how individuals interact with one another. An organization's participants must constantly link their work to the goals of the organization.

Focus on process by focusing on performance. An organization's participants link what they do to how they perform. Process without achievement is insufficient in a competitive environment that demands dramatic turnarounds. True, change may not occur overnight, but individuals need signposts to assure them that they are on the right path and heading toward where they want to go. Recent lessons from teaching may help guide how individuals are to perform within the organization. We know that epiphanies do not happen to the majority of students we teach. Progress may be slow, but it can be constant. Individuals teach not for one standardized test, but instead to constantly monitor progress. At the end of every class I frequently administer a 1-minute "exam" that asks students the major lesson they learned in class. I have students write short papers throughout the term and use my comments to help them improve the next paper. I offer constant formative comments that ultimately end in a summative note about their progress over the term.

It is possible to approach organizational life in much the same manner. An organization's participants have a sense of the goals they want to achieve and how they will know they have succeeded. They have a time frame, either self-imposed or constructed with external influences (such as deadlines for grant applications, tenure cycles, or beginnings and endings of school years), and they establish markers along the way that will tell them how they are doing. A focus on performance will change the processes in which individuals are involved. Since the organization works in a decentralized environment with an overall sense of what they are about, those who are most intimately involved in the process are responsible for monitoring performance, suggesting changes to the processes, and gauging success.

Performance is also something that needs to be clear and understandable to those who are not directly involved in the process. In effect, an organization cannot simply say, "We are doing a really good job," and expect that everyone must accept the statement by blind faith. Indicators of excellence are essential. Because everyone is tied to the overall goals of the organization and exhibits concern toward one another, they also say something more than simply reporting numbers on a page. An academic community is involved in intellectual undertakings, so at times a group's achievements may not have a "bottom line." Instead they have frameworks for discussion, in much the same way that evaluative processes in some schools eschew simple grades and attend to narratives that point out areas of strengths, weaknesses, and improvement.

Focus on performance by focusing on improvement. Herein lies one of the central tenets of reengineering. An organization's participants are never satisfied with simply achieving what they set out to achieve. An organization set up for change is fundamentally different from one that seeks the status quo. Those organizations that exist in a stable environment where change is not necessary simply regurgitate processes over and over. Those involved in dynamic change constantly monitor how to improve processes and how to improve performance.

They may well have reached an enrollment goal or a fiscal goal or a departmental goal, but they may have expended too many resources or spent too much time or too much energy in meeting the goal. Instead, individuals search out ways to improve what they do by returning to the processes they use to achieve performance and rethink how changes in the larger environment may afford opportunities we had not considered. They bring in people unfamiliar with their processes to offer constructive criticism by way of cultural audits so that people who see the world differently from theirs are able to offer ideas for improvement. They seek commentary from colleagues in other arenas of the organization who may see the group's work differently from themselves.

And too, everyone focuses on results. However, bigger is not always better. If individuals achieve one numerical goal such as enrollment projections, it does not necessarily mean they want to improve by having more students. All areas should not grow every year; instead, resources might be diverted from one area to another for a particular strategic rationale that has been communicated throughout the organization. And improvement is not simply numerical formulas. They also are capable of improving the quality of work and its output. Again, when individuals move away from simplistic "bottom lines" and toward narrative discussions about what they are attempting to do, they also open up possibilities for considering ways to improve results as well. Improvement from this perspective affords the organization the opportunity, for example, of not merely applauding a student when he or she finishes a dissertation but discovering ways that students might complete a superb study, one that wins an award, and is used either in a theoretical or practical sense.

Focus on improvement by focusing on results. An organization cannot improve if the individuals do not have some sense of what they hope to achieve. Achievements are marked by clearly delineated goals that are understood without interpretive commentary from those involved in the process. Because organizations are unique entities, more than likely they will have criteria for excellence and achievement that are different from unit to unit and from organization to organization. Without such clarity, they are simply involved in processes that provide no sense of organizational glue or understanding about purpose.

Results have three critical points. Those nearest to the tasks develop the results in discussion with others within the organization. The results have a clear endpoint on which to be measured. The results are capable of measurement; albeit the measures may not be standardized tests or traditional measurable formats.

We have arrived, then, at circular foci. Such circular activity once again moves individuals away from compartmentalized or hierarchical thinking and action, where one is involved in one segmented process and someone else does another. No one sees the entire picture or has a sense about how the parts fit the whole. Instead, in a reengineered organization individuals constantly move from one act to another and back again so that they consider what they are about, what they want to achieve, how they want to gauge their achievements, and how they might improve by what they are about, what they want to achieve, and so on (see Table 6.1).

Such thinking is impossible or frustrating in a traditional organization where individuals hold standard goals and objectives and strategies in line with mechanistic metaphors of performance. If the organization's participants are to implement what they hope to undertake with circular foci, then they must move beyond the box in which academic life is currently framed and toward a different organizational framework.

Getting Out of the Box

Redesign Rather Than Tinker

Fundamental change is more difficult, time-consuming, and risky than tidying up a few processes that appear messy. As Hammer and Champy (1993) note:

TABLE 6.1 Redesigning Colleges and Universities

	Traditional Organization	*Learning Organization*
Structure	Hierarchical Rigid Centralized Individual focus Formal boundaries	Flat Fluid Decentralized Team focus Boundary spanning

Values	Competition
	Status quo
	Individual focus
	Structure
	Nonresponsive to external
	    constituencies
		Cooperation
		Experimentation
		Community focused
		Culture
		Responsive to the people
		    served

Decision-Making	Leader-driven
	Unitary problem-solving
	Bureaucratic; emphasis on
	    reporting lines
	
	Goals defined by imme-
	    diate problem
	Militaristic metaphor of
	    strategic planning
		Team-driven
		Systemic reform
		Soft projects; emphasis on
		    problem identification
		    and solution
		Goals defined by mission
		
		Cultural metaphor of
		    redesign

Organizations often go to great trouble and expense to avoid the radical redesign associated with reengineering. They may reorganize, which means that they don't change work processes at all, only the administrative boxes around the people doing it. Companies downsize, which just means using fewer people to do the same or less work in the same way. Companies try motivational programs, which use incentives to try to get people to work harder. (p. 202)

The problem is that what most of us in academe have been doing is fixing a flawed process rather than rethinking the process itself. Think of any number of examples I have offered and how we might tinker with the problem rather than redesign it.

- An institution's revenues fall unexpectedly. A freeze is put on travel funds for faculty, and the admissions office is told to increase enrollment.

- An accreditation visit points out that the management of off-campus centers is unclear. A committee is formed to study the problem.

- A study reveals that minority students feel disenfranchised. The president proclaims that one day in the spring will be Diversity Day.
- A state legislator desires greater proof that faculty are working. The administration develops a survey about faculty workloads that provides evidence that they are working.
- The academic senate decides that more emphasis needs to be placed on teaching excellence. A professor is relieved from teaching two courses and establishes a "Center for Teaching Excellence" without any budget.

Each example underscores the problems with tinkering, and the more significant task that awaits those who desire to reengineer. I might also add that each example derives from the "real world" of an institution where I have either consulted or visited. In many respects, the manner in which the organization's participants dealt with their problems is entirely understandable—and flawed. Although I consider myself efficient, there are times when I need to stop and think about what is the root cause of a problem, rather than merely find the nearest bandage to cover the wound. Efficiency often obscures real problems or delays the day of reckoning. A spring day that deals with diversity may well be one step in a positive direction, just as the creation of a center for teaching may be necessary. But if the organization's participants are serious about issues such as diversity or teaching and learning, then they need to attend to such issues over a significant time period with substantial cultural and intellectual resources.

The examples I provided above point out how organizations suffering from attention deficit disorder respond. An issue rises to the surface, and individuals must deal with it. When the next crisis of the day arises, the organization is ready. Sometimes the proposed solutions actually solve a problem. Off-campus programs often have unclear management schemas and a committee may come up with viable solutions to untangle confused reporting lines. If the intent of faculty workload reports is to get the state legislature off the institution's case, then the development of a report may be perfect.

And yet, none of the solutions go to the core of the problems that face the institution. How to define teaching excellence or how to develop a community that honors diversity or how to develop creative off-campus programming so that it is more than an appendage to the institution are issues that call for long-term redesign. Note that what the institution needs to do is commit cultural and intellectual resources rather than fiscal resources. Yes, change costs money. The clearest way to stymie change is also to say that the problem certainly exists, but they do not have any money to solve it.

But individuals fool themselves if they believe that simply throwing money at a problem prompts a solution. Prior to the commitment of funds, they need to invest their own personal and organizational energies in moving them beyond the confines of where they are, beyond the box. If they do not do so, then the problems will simply reoccur, or as noted earlier, they will develop solutions that are "good enough," rather than focus on excellence, improvement, and achievement.

Paint the Whole Picture: Think Big

What will make a difference in colleges and universities that seek to actively prepare for the demands of the 21st century is the comprehensive nature of the procedures of reengineering. Individuals "think big" in two ways. One challenge lies in the ability to move beyond a concern for simply the unit or area in which the individual resides. For faculty members the struggle will be to expend as much cultural energy orienting them to the nature of the institution as graduate schools and professional associations do in orienting them to the discipline. For midlevel administrators the task will be to help them move beyond the assumption that whatever they do in their area is fine and it has little relation to other units or overall goals. In effect, what had been expected of college and university presidents and few others, a vision of the organization, is now what must be developed, shared, and nurtured by all the organization's participants.

True, different groups and individuals respond in different manners and have unique capabilities. An organization ought not expect of the young assistant professor or new staff worker in student affairs what they expect of an individual who holds an endowed chair in humanities or the provost. But for too long an organization's participants have seen one another's jobs as unrelated to another or to the overall organizational fabric. To move beyond standard thinking everyone needs to realize that they are all involved in the creation of the organization rather than assuming that presidents alone are the visionaries.

The other way individuals think big is by developing and improving on significant goals and challenges. An organization does not always need numerical gains to think big. In an intellectual organization what indi-

TABLE 6.2 Organizational Redesign As Defined by Key Organizational Factors

	Traditional	*Responsive*
Mission	Not widely understood, used for public relations	Wide agreement and belief in by internal constituencies
Faculty Work	Expectations similar for everyone	Framework remains, but wide leeway exists based on individual strengths and communal needs
Organizational Structure	Formalized, organized around functions	Fluid, organized to solve problems, identify new possibilities
Relationship to Environment	Nonresponsive; sharp differentiation across sectors	Responsive; greater flexibility and communication across sectors

viduals hope to do is develop processes and results that meet high standards and are explainable and demonstrable to constituencies beyond the specific area. The phrase "good enough" is not part of the vocabulary of an organization involved in redesign.

A high performance organization is like any exceptional piece of art. Individuals do not look to the organization and point to one component of the work; rather, the piece in its entirety is what makes it remarkable. True, we may see *Romeo and Juliet* and marvel at the acting of one or another actor, or we may admire the choreography in a performance of *Swan Lake*; such parts of a piece may deserve applause but our admiration for the entire work may be muted because the scenery in one, or the acting in another, is not as good as the rest. What makes for exceptionality is when every aspect of the work is superb.

The kinds of colleges and universities I am speaking of function in the same way. When we investigate the organization, it is not merely that the president is capable and talented, or that the faculty has a handful of individuals who have won prestigious awards as first-rate intellectuals. Rather, wherever we look we find greatness, and as we continue to look we find that the organization's participants not only find excellence, they *expect* it (see Table 6.2).

Paint the Whole Picture: Work Small

It is all fine and good to use elaborate language about vision and greatness, but when I arrive at work in the morning I need to put dreams and big pictures into action. I do not suggest that individuals should leave their visions behind once they get to work. Indeed, if this book has been about anything, it has been focused on creating and maintaining connections across organizational identity, ideals, and day-to-day actions. Nevertheless, I all too often have met individuals who are unable to create connections between big ideas and small actions. Either they are dreamers without feet planted on the ground, or they are so wedded to action that they cannot lift their eyes to the heavens to see what might be seen.

In a redesigned organization, the individuals attend to details. Everyone's input is valued and deemed necessary for improvement. I have been at institutions where senior administrators worry about how students are treated and want to improve on concerns such as advising. They create a task force composed of a group of faculty and a vice president for student affairs. What they neglect when they act in this manner is the signal that is sent, and the input that is lost.

Before students get to a professor, more often than not they need to speak with a secretary; before students try to register for courses, they usually ask secretaries for advice about how to register online or how to short-circuit one cumbersome process or another. But how often do we invite secretaries to participate in strategy sessions or other organizational meetings? When decision-makers omit staff from discussions about improvement, they miss out on the staff's wisdom and input. And as troubling, leaders also send a signal that the staff's advice is not necessary or desired. In effect, those in structural leadership positions create a sector of the academic community that learns implicitly that their job is to stick to the details and not proffer suggestions for improvement.

If the organization is to "work small," then everyone needs information about the organization. All individuals are encouraged to offer suggestions and advice about how they might go about improving their work, or how the work of others might foster or impede their own jobs. If individuals are capable of fostering an environment in which attention to detail is pointed out as essential, and such attention is tied into the larger framework in which they function, then the organization's vision will be grounded and comprehensible, rather than merely flowery language divorced from the work of those who toil in the fields every day. People need more than rhetoric; they need rhetoric that becomes reality in those everyday fields.

Own a Compass

"A company must have a core ideology," write Collins and Porras (1994). "It must also have an unrelenting drive for progress. And finally, it must be well designed as an organization to preserve the core and stimulate progress, with all the key pieces working in alignment" (Collins & Porras, 1994, p. 218). In other words, have a sense of the organization's identity and culture and ensure that actions fit the ideology, or seek to change the ideology. To ignore culture and ideology is to throw reengineering to the wind.

An organization's culture means that what is right for one's college may be wrong for another university. How one group defines productive faculty may be different from how another group defines productive professors. I am not saying that what exists in the environment is to be ignored, to the contrary. However, the manner in which the organization's participants read the environment and develop actions needs to be in sync with who they are, rather than merely assume the mantle of a chameleon and change whenever the colors of the environment change. We are involved in long-term systemic change; not the momentary solution that has consumed our short-term memory.

Similarly, how the organization rewards productive faculty needs to be aligned with their cultural definitions. The compass spins aimlessly when individuals say one thing and do another. If they honestly want to focus on local community issues then faculty need to be encouraged through incentives to focus on such issues. Individuals can no longer say they want better town-grown relations, for example, but penalize the professor who works in the schools or homeless shelter and reward the jet setter who speaks at international conferences. Conversely, if the organization wants to reward those faculty who pursue theoretical research, then they need to provide them with support and incentives to do so and not look askance when they develop agendas and proposals that will take them far afield.

The compass, self-created, monitored, and corrected, guides organizational action. The compass has a history of its own, but it also comes without an owner's manual. We know it is precious, we accept that it will help guide organizational actions, and the participants take care of it. Without it, we are lost.

Conclusion

In many respects organizational redesign is a study in contrasts. Individuals recognize that change of this sort will take years to accomplish, but they also seek immediate results. They reject total quality management as an endpoint, but utilize it as an approach to get where they are going and to gauge how successful they are. They need to stick to a plan and hold on to it regardless of external forces, but they also need to constantly monitor the environment and their constituencies to ensure they are on the right path and do not need to make corrections. The organization's participants highlight the importance of culture, but also accept it as a living text rather than the received word. Culture is dynamic, not static, so everyone takes part in reflective conversations in order to ensure they hold on to principles rather than whimsically drop them. Individuals provide greater power and voice in a decentralized system than they have before, but they also emphasize their core beliefs and ideologies. While the organization encourages people to make decisions and work autonomously, they also do not reside in an atmosphere where "anything goes." Individuals acknowledge the import of leadership, and at the same time lessen the traditional notion of its authority and power. They reject the militaristic imagery of strategy while they develop new ones.

Such paradoxes, even contradictions, may seem like an invitation to become involved in a long, difficult, somewhat chaotic undertaking. The orderly nature of organizational life that has existed throughout much of this century, where everyone knows his or her place and lines of authority are clear enough to be charted on a nice, neat chart, are no longer. Instead, we find ourselves following unclear maps, involved in constant dialogue with one another, and engaged in frequently difficult conversations about whether we are meeting one another's and the organization's needs, and whether our actions support the core values of the institution.

Do we have to redesign? Are such seemingly epic struggles worth it? The answer is yes to both questions. The future demands new academic organizations. Our creation of them involves us in a great tradition of building and maintaining academic excellence and being responsive to those whom we serve.

Frequently Asked Questions

I have had friends and colleagues read parts of this book as I have written it, and I have discussed different ideas at conferences and in lectures as a consultant to colleges and universities. I also teach a doctoral seminar on administration that is composed of midlevel administrators at a variety of different postsecondary institutions. I have used drafts of this book in class for feedback and debate. Certain questions continually arise and deserve a response.

I thought you were politically on the left. Isn't reengineering just another way for managers to assert more authority over the faculty and staff?

I am on the left, yes. Organizational redesign is neither anti-democratic nor warmed-over Taylorism. If anything, redesign offers a way for broader participation and decision making on the part of multiple groups and constituencies. At the same time, we also ought not fool ourselves that reengineering as a structure or any structure ensures democratic participation in an organization. Organizations exist through human activity and ideas. Just as it is possible for individuals to subvert democratic efforts within a democracy, it will also be possible for institutional leaders to claim that reengineering is necessary and choose some ideas that enhance their power and overlook others. As I noted, what is necessary in each institution that reengineers is to define organizational commitments and goals, as I did in the introduction. Such commitments provide definition. Unlike Taylorism or "great man" theories of leadership, reengineering at least sets the stage for possible wide-scale decentralized efforts by all of an organization's participants.

But don't ideas like soft projects and the lessening of departmental structure set the stage for greater administrative authority? It sounds anti-union.

Not at all. We must appreciate the necessary tension that exists across constituencies. Some, but not all, colleges and universities have unions that successfully represent the interests of different constituencies. I have been to campuses where unions are helpful, and I have visited other campuses where they are not. Many campuses also are not unionized. Unions, like reengineering, are empty concepts if they are not defined and contextualized. If unionization means the rigid definition of structure that maintains at all costs the status quo regardless of present contexts, then I fully understand how reengineering can be seen as problematic.

But few unions exist on campuses that do not recognize the dramatic changes taking place in society that demand colleges and universities to reorganize how we work. Organizational redesign is not, however, a code word for "downsizing," which in itself is a 1990s code word for "firing." If anything, reengineering provides all constituencies with the possibility for greater participation in deciding what work they do and how it is done. Our tasks may well be reorganized, but such reorganizations are done via full participation of those involved in the processes.

OK, fine, but elsewhere you've derided organizational fads. How come you speak of this one with such fervor as if it's a panacea for all that ails us?

If I have been interpreted as saying that redesign or reengineering is a panacea, then I have been misunderstood. It is not a path to utopia, the New Jerusalem, or any other promised land. It is not a magic elixir. However, it is unlike previous management gimmicks in two fundamental ways. First, reengineering provides a way to break out of traditional molds. Whereas TQM, strategic planning, and the like sought to improve upon present day practices, redesign seeks to change fundamentally such practices. We don't tinker with what we do, we change it.

Second, I have always felt that some of these ideas that are borrowed from business demand an organizational contortionist in order to fit them to academe. Colleges and universities are special places. They are different from for-profit businesses with "bottom lines." Nevertheless, in an era when dramatic change is needed, it is not helpful to suggest that our leaders either have to go with their intuition, since nothing from the business world will work, or use ideas for organizations entirely different from ours. Reengineering is intellectually driven and appears to be a perfect fit for organizations that have a history of shared governance and collegial decision-making.

That's fine to say, but I don't think you understand the pressures everyone faces right now. I have faculty who need training in technology and I have to get the place wired so that everyone can interface with the library's new electronic gizmos; I don't have time to redesign.

You've just answered why we need to. I fully appreciate the pressures we face. Everyone, not just the faculty, is facing new challenges in the workplace as they recognize the need for changed infrastructures, among other things. We have two choices. We can muddle through and continue to feel like the Mad Hatter in *Alice in Wonderland* screaming, "no time, no time." Although we will accomplish some tasks in this manner, we will end up exhausted, burned out, and incapable of dealing strategically with comprehensive reform.

Or we can take a breath and consider how to redesign processes so that individuals and groups work with one another across functions and structures in a cohesive manner.

You don't get it. I can't just put the brakes on everything for a year and say we're going to reengineer and let everything come to a halt.

I never said that everything should come to a halt. Think of it in two ways. First, when we run a marathon we don't just wake up and say, "I'm going to drop everything; I'm going to run 26 miles today." We train. Different people train in different ways, and depending on the shape we're in, we might begin very slowly or relatively quickly. Organizational redesign is similar. We don't drop everything. Reengineering is a process, and processes occur over time.

Second, we learn about reengineering and educate the institution about it. We don't simply get the reengineering bug and begin. We discuss the idea with our colleagues. We raise and debate issues. We create study groups that set agendas. Remember, reengineering will never work if it is the brainchild of a single individual. It takes an organization to bring about reengineering.

OK, you've got me. How do I begin?

You just did.

References

Adams, C., & Peck, T. (1996, September). Process redesign. *Executive Excellence*, p. 14-15.

American Association of University Professors (1985). Academic freedom and tenure: Statement of Principles, 1940. In M. Finkelstein (Ed.), *Ashe reader on faculty and faculty issues in colleges and universities*, pp. 143-145. Lexington, MA: Ginn.

Argyris, C. (1991). Teaching smart people how to learn. *Harvard Business Review, 69*(3), 99-109

Belasco, J. A., & Stayer, R. C. (1993). *Flight of the buffalo: Soaring to excellence, learning to let employees lead.* New York: Warner Books.

Belasco, J. A. (1990). *Teaching the elephant to dance: The manager's guide to empowering change.* New York: Plume.

Bennis, W., & Mische, M. (1996, September). 21st century organization. *Executive Excellence,* p. 7-8.

Block, P. (1987). *The empowered manager: Positive political skills at work.* San Francisco: Jossey-Bass.

Bloom, A. (1987). *The closing of the American mind: How higher education has failed democracy and impoverished the souls of today's students.* New York: Simon & Schuster.

Boyer, E. (1990). *Scholarship reconsidered: Priorities for the professoriate.* Princeton, NJ: Carnegie Foundation for the Advancement of Teaching.

Cameron, K. (1978). Measuring organizational effectiveness in institutions of higher education. *Administrative Science Quarterly, 23,* 604-629.

Cameron, K., & Whetten, D. (1996). Organizational effectiveness and quality: The second generation. In J. C. Smart (Ed.), *Higher education: Handbook of theory and research* (Vol. 11, pp. 265-306). New York: Agathon Press.

Carlyle, T. (1897). *Heroes and hero-worship.* London: Chapman and Hall.

Chaffee, E. E., & Tierney, W. G. (1988). *Collegiate culture and leadership strategies.* New York: Macmillan.

Chaffee, E. E. (1998). Listening to the people we serve. In W. G. Tierney (Ed.), *The responsive university: Restructuring for high performance.* Baltimore: Johns Hopkins University Press.

Champy, J. (1995). *Reengineering management: The mandate for new leadership.* New York: Harper Business.

Chickering, A. W., & Gamson, Z. F. (1987, March). Seven principles for good practice in undergraduate education. *AAHE Bulletin,* 3-7.

Clark, B. (1980). The organizational saga in higher education. In H. Leavitt (Ed.), *Readings in managerial psychology.* Chicago: Chicago University Press.

Clark, B. (1983). *The higher education system: Academic organization in cross-national perspective.* Los Angeles: University of California Press.

College Board (1993, September). Trends in student aid: 1983-93. Washington, DC: The College Entrance Examination Board.

Collier, J., Jr. (1973). *Alaskan Eskimo education: A film analysis of cultural confrontation in the schools.* Chicago: Holt, Rinehart & Winston.

Collins, J. C., & Porras, J. I. (1994). *Built to last: Successful habits of visionary companies.* New York: Harper Business.

Collins, P. H. (1991). *Black feminist thought: Knowledge, consciousness and the politics of empowerment.* New York: Routledge.

Conrad, C. (Ed.). (1985). *Access to quality undergraduate education.* Atlanta, GA: Southern Region Education Board.

Council for Aid to Education (1997). *Breaking the social contract: The fiscal crisis in California higher education.* New York: Author.

Drucker, P. F. (1990). *Managing the non-profit organization: Principles and practices.* New York: Harper Business.

Duderstadt, J. (1997, July). Revolutionary changes: Understanding the challenges and the possibilities. *Business Officer,* p. 1-15.

Francis, C. (1990, July/August). Student aid: Is it working like it is supposed to? *Change, 22*(4), 35-42.

Gappa, J. M. (1996). Off the tenure track: Six models for full-time, non-tenurable appointments (AAHE forum on faculty roles and rewards working paper series). Washington, DC: American Association for Higher Education.

Garvin, D. A. (1991). Building a learning organization. *Harvard Business Review, 71*(4), 78-91.

Geiger, R. L. (1993). *Research and relevant knowledge: American research universities since World War II.* New York: Oxford University Press.

Goleman, D. (1990, June 21). The fidgets aren't just in childhood: Adults with troubles are learning. *New York Times,* B6.

Goodstein, D. (1994, August 31). The coming dark age of U.S. research. *Los Angeles Times (Commentary),* p. B7.

Hammer, M., & Champy, J. (1993). *Reengineering the corporation: A manifesto for business revolution.* New York: Harper Business.

Handy, C. (1990). *The age of unreason.* Boston: Harvard Business School Press.

Hauptman, A. (1990). *The college tuition spiral.* Washington, DC: American Council on Education.

Haworth, J. G., & Conrad, C. F. (1997). *Quality in higher education: Developing and sustaining high-quality programs.* Boston: Allyn and Bacon.

Hearn, J.C., & Longanecker, D. (1985). Enrollment effects of alternative postsecondary pricing policies. *Journal of Higher Education, 56*(5), 458-508.

Johnstone, D. B. (1996, Autumn). Learning productivity: Some key questions. *Learning Productivity News, 1*(2), p. 1-3.

Katz, M. (1987). *Reconstructing American education.* Cambridge, MA: Harvard University Press.

Katzenbach, J. R., & Smith, D. K. (1994). *The wisdom of teams: Creating the high-performance organization.* New York: Harper Business.

Keller, G. (1983). *Academic strategy: The management revolution in American higher education.* Baltimore: Johns Hopkins University Press.

Keith, K. M. (1996). *Qualifying examination.* Los Angeles: University of Southern California, School of Education.

Kouzes, J. M., & Posner, B. Z. (1993). *Credibility: How leaders gain and lose it, why people demand it.* San Francisco: Jossey-Bass.

Kouzes, J. M., & Posner, B. Z. (1987). *The leadership challenge: How to get extraordinary things done in organizations.* San Francisco: Jossey-Bass.

Lawler, E. E., III. (1986). *High-involvement management.* San Francisco: Jossey-Bass.

Layzell, D. T. (1996). Faculty workload and productivity: Recurrent issues with new imperatives. *Review of Higher Education, 19*(3), 267-281.

Leslie, D. W., & Fretwell, E. K., Jr. (1996). *Wise moves in hard times: Creating and managing resilient colleges and universities.* San Francisco: Jossey-Bass.

Levin, H. M. (1991). Raising productivity in higher education. *Journal of Higher Education, 62*(3), 242-262.

March, J., & Cohen, M. (1974). *Leadership and ambiguity.* New York: McGraw-Hill.

Massy, W., & Wilger, A. (1995, July/August). Improving productivity: What faculty think about it and its effect on quality. *Change, 27*(4), 10-20.

Mayhew, L. B. (1979). *Surviving the eighties.* San Francisco: Jossey-Bass.

Mintzberg, H. (1994). The fall and rise of strategic planning. *Harvard Business Review 72* (1), 107-115.

Mintzberg, H. (1987a). The strategy concept I: Five Ps for strategy. *California Management Review, 30*(1), 11-24.

Mintzberg, H. (1987b). The strategy concept II: Another look at why organizations need strategies. *California Management Review, 30*(1), 25-32.

Mishel, L., & Bernstein, J. (1994). *The state of working America.* Washington, DC: Economic Policy Institute.

Moore, K. (1983). The structure of presidents' and deans' careers. *Journal of Higher Education, 54*(5), 500-515.

Moore, W. (1971). *Blind man on a freeway.* San Francisco: Jossey-Bass.

Mumper, M. (1996). Removing college price barriers: What government has done and why it hasn't worked. Albany, NY: SUNY.

Nanus, B. (1992). *Visionary leadership.* San Francisco: Jossey-Bass.

National Commission on Responsibilities for Financing Postsecondary Education. (1993). *Making college affordable again.* Washington, DC: National Commission on Responsibilities for Financing Postsecondary Education.

Noble, D. (1994). Let them eat skills. *The Review of Education/Pedagogy/Cultural Studies 16*(1), 15-29.

Onions, C. T. (1966). *The Oxford dictionary of English etymology.* Oxford, England: Oxford University Press.

Peters, T. J., & Waterman, R. H., Jr. (1982). *In search of excellence: Lessons from America's best-run companies.* New York: Harper & Row.

Pondy, L. (1978). Leadership is a language game. In M. McCall & M. Lombardo (Eds.), *Leadership: Where else can we go?*, Durham, NC: Duke University Press.

Quinn, J. B. (1993, November 15). The taxpayers vs. higher ed. *Newsweek*, p. 51.

RAND. (1997). *Breaking the social contract: The fiscal crisis in higher education.* Santa Monica, CA: RAND Corporation.

Ray, C. A. (1986). Corporate culture: The last frontier of control. *Journal of Management Studies, 23*(3), 287-297.

Reich, R. (1992). *The work of nations.* New York: Vintage Books.

Rice, R. E. (1996). *Making a place for the American scholar.* (AAHE Forum on Faculty Roles and Rewards Working Paper Series). Washington, DC: American Association for Higher Education.

Risen, J. (1994, September). Reich says jobs fail to offset wage, income inequality. *Los Angeles Times,* p. A27.

Ruben, B. (Ed.). (1995). *Quality in higher education.* New Brunswick, NJ: Transaction Publishers.

Sacks, P. (1996). *Generation X goes to college: An eye-opening account of teaching in postmodern America.* Chicago: Open Court.

Senge, P. M. (1990). *The fifth discipline: The art and practice of the learning organization.* New York: Doubleday Currency.

Stiehm, J. (1994). Diversity's diversity. In David Theo Goldberg (Ed.), *Multiculturalism* (p. 140-156). London: Basil Blackwell.

Tierney, W. G. (Ed.). (In press). *Faculty productivity: Facts, fictions and issues.* New York: Garland Publishing.

Tierney, W. G. (Ed.) (1998). *The responsive university: Restructuring for high performance.* Baltimore, MD: Johns Hopkins University Press.

Tierney, W. G. (1997). Tenure and community in academe. *Educational Researcher,* 26(8), 17-23.

Tierney, W. G. (1994). *Building communities of difference: Higher education in the twenty-first century.* Westport, CT: Bergin and Garvey.

Tierney, W. G. (1993). Academic freedom and the parameters of knowledge. *Harvard Educational Review,* 63,(2), 145-159.

Tierney, W. G. (1989). *Curricular landscapes, democratic vistas: Transformative leadership in higher education.* Westport, CT: Praeger.

Tierney, W. G. (1988). *The web of leadership: The presidency in higher education.* Greenwich, CT: JAI Press.

Tierney, W. G., & Bensimon, E. M. (1996). *Promotion and tenure: Community and socialization in academe.* Albany, NY: State University of New York Press.

Wender, P. M. (1990, June 21). A life spent out of focus. *New York Times,* p. B6.

Whalen, E. L. (1991). *Responsibility center budgeting: An approach to decentralized management of institutions of higher education.* Indianapolis, IN: Indiana University Press.

Index

About the Author

William G. Tierney is the Wilbur-Kieffer Professor of Higher Education and Director of the Center for Higher Education Policy Analysis at the University of Southern California. He holds advanced degrees from Harvard and Stanford Universities and a BA from Tufts University. His most recent book is *The Responsive University: Restructuring for High Performance* (1998). He is currently involved in a 4-year study pertaining to faculty roles and rewards. He recently received the distinguished research award from the Association for the Study of Higher Education, and *Change* magazine recognized him as one of 40 young leaders in the academy.